SHAPING GERMAN FOREIGN POLICY

SHAPING GERMAN FOREIGN POLICY

History, Memory, and National Interest

Anika Leithner

FIRST**FORUM**PRESS

BOULDER & LONDON

Published in the United States of America in 2009 by
FirstForumPress
A division of Lynne Rienner Publishers, Inc.
1800 30th Street, Boulder, Colorado 80301
www.firstforumpress.com

and in the United Kingdom by
FirstForumPress
A division of Lynne Rienner Publishers, Inc.
3 Henrietta Street, Covent Garden, London WC2E 8LU

Library of Congress Cataloging-in-Publication Data
Leithner, Anika, 1977–
Shaping German foreign policy : history, memory, and national interest /
Anika Leithner.
Includes bibliographical references and index.
ISBN 978-1-935049-00-5 (hardcover : alk. paper)
1. Germany—Foreign relations—1945– 2. Historiography—Germany. 3.
National socialism—Psychological aspects. I. Title.
JZ1592.L45 2009
327.43—dc22   2008033609

British Cataloguing in Publication Data
A Cataloguing in Publication record for this book
is available from the British Library.

This book was produced from digital files prepared by the author
using the FirstForumComposer.

Printed and bound in the United States of America

 The paper used in this publication meets the requirements
of the American National Standard for Permanence of
Paper for Printed Library Materials Z39.48-1992.

5 4 3 2

Gra, Disleacht, agus Cairdeas

This book is dedicated to my husband, Erin P. Clemons

Filia est pars parentis

Dieses Buch ist meinen Eltern
Doris und Gerald Leithner, gedwidmet

Contents

Figures and Tables

Acknowledgments

First and foremost, I thank my husband, Erin P. Clemons. I do not know who I would be without him. *Mo anam cara!*

I also owe a great debt of gratitude to my mentor, Professor Francis A. Beer. I first met him at a time in my life when I had almost convinced myself that I was not an academic. Luckily, he saw in me what I had yet to discover myself. I am not exaggerating when I say that his example and his intellectual guidance have changed my path in life as fundamentally as only a truly great teacher can.

I would like to thank all my colleagues at the California Polytechnic State University. They exemplify the term collegiality, and I am delighted to find myself in such wonderful company. In particular, I am grateful to Ron den Otter for his unwavering friendship and support (and for countless UFC nights). I also thank Craig Arceneaux for being such a great friend and mentor (and for the "Old Vienna Inn").

Thanks to everyone at FirstForumPress for their help in the publication of this book. I am especially grateful to Lynne Rienner for believing in me and for enabling me to share my work with a larger audience.

Finally, I need to thank my parents, Gerald and Doris Leithner for everything they have done for me. I could not be prouder to be my parents' daughter. I am also grateful to my brothers, Dominik and Sebastian, and to my grandmothers, Herta and Hermine. They all have supported and shaped me in too many ways to count.

For any individuals whom I may have forgotten to mention, please accept my sincere thanks.

1

Introduction: Historical Memory in German Foreign Policy

"I often hear foreigners say what they would do if they had Germany's wealth, its size or its population. I never hear them say what they would do if they had Germany's past."[1] – Senior German Diplomat

It is difficult to think of another country that is as obsessed with its own recent history as Germany is. While "[m]ost countries celebrate the best in their pasts ... Germany unrelentingly promotes its worst."[2] Even sixty years after the end of World War II, lengthy and almost ritualized debates about the lessons of history and what it means to be German after Hitler take place in abundance, as perhaps most famously evidenced by the so-called *Historikerstreit* (historians' battle) about the importance of remembrance during the mid-1990s. Books written about the topic are almost guaranteed to become national bestsellers, even those that portray the entire German people as a historically anti-Semitic bunch whose natural inclination to commit mass murder made them perfect candidates to become Hitler's "willing executioners." Documentaries about the Holocaust – and the war in general – enjoy some of the highest TV ratings and air on a regular basis on any of the main networks. Films such as *Schindler's List* were sold out weeks in advance and visits to the movie theater in order to see it became mandatory field trips for most German high schools in 1994. Indeed, history classes in Germany tend to spend a disproportionate amount of time teaching about the events of the World War II and its meaning for present-day Germany. Even German politics remain heavily influenced by the "past that will not pass."[3]

This book answers the question of how (and how much) the past continues to shape German foreign policy behavior at the beginning of the 21st century. Unlike traditional approaches, which focus mainly on external, structural factors as explanatory valuables, I make a case for history – or more specifically, historical memory – as a central feature in foreign policy analysis. In particular, the complex relationship between historical memory, interests, identity, and foreign policy behavior holds the key to understanding German security decisions today.

I should point out that the view of history I adopt here is based on the notion that all knowledge of history is subjective. This is not to say that there are no objective historical facts, but rather that the way observers remember those facts and the lessons they draw from them are open to interpretation and re-interpretation. While it may be too far-fetched to think of history in general as "just another discourse,[4]" it seems reasonable to argue that historical memory is indeed largely discursive in nature.

On the basis of this assumption, the main argument in this book is that while German foreign policy is still shaped by the historical memory of World War II, the exact nature of this memory is slowly changing as the lessons of history are being reinterpreted in such a way as to allow German leaders to reconcile the legacy of World War II – which has become so much part of German national identity and has in turn affected the concept of national interest – with the demands of a post-Cold War world. Germany appears to be on the road to normalcy, at least with regard to its views on the practice of foreign policy, but that road is long and change remains incremental rather than abrupt. German foreign policy is following a historical path, and where it has been in the past very much defines where it can go it the future, and how quickly it can get there.

The Interaction of Political Thought, Talk, and Action

Germany has – for obvious reasons – been under intense scrutiny ever since the end of World War II,[5] but following the country's return to full sovereignty and its re-unification in 1990, a veritable boom of analyses about the future of Germany's foreign policy occurred. The new Germany was much too large and much too powerful for the rest of the world to ignore.[6] Even as Germans were celebrating on top of the Berlin Wall, speculations began about the consequences these recent developments would have for Germany, Europe, and the entire international community. Most observers expected significant changes to result from Germany's more powerful position.[7]

At the heart of most debates was the question of how the end of the Cold War would affect German attitudes toward the use of force as a foreign policy tool. Some subscribed to the "normalization" thesis, which suggested that because the nature of the international system "explains the generation of military power in all countries, without regard to their internal societies,"[8] Germany should be expected to pursue a much less reticent foreign policy now that the external constraints of the Cold War had been removed. As a result, the country would begin to focus much more on strategic interests, seize advantage of the new position of power it found itself in vis-à-vis the rest of

Europe, inevitably build up its military potential, and simultaneously lose any hesitations it may have had about using force to achieve its goals. As a result, the rest of Europe would either balance against a strong new Germany,[9] possibly leading to the "Balkanization" of Europe and the resurgence of nationalism,[10] or Europe would form an anti-American alliance around a German core.[11] At the very least, Germany would attempt to increase its power, strive for a more unilateral and less antimilitarist foreign policy, and become generally more assertive in international politics.[12]

Since these predictions were derived from the belief that a country's foreign policy is largely determined by external factors, they naturally posited that a significant change in Germany's external environment, i.e. the end of the Cold War, would lead to significant changes in its foreign policy behavior. Most of these predictions have not occurred.

At the other end of the spectrum were those who predicted that German foreign policy behavior would not change very much after reunification, arguing that Germany would remain a "tamed power"[13] and continue to pursue the "same policies and patterns of behavior [it] had followed for the past forty years."[14] Proponents of this "continuity" thesis argued that Germany had learned the lessons of its troubled past and absorbed them into German political culture. These lessons became so entrenched in German ideology that even an abrupt change in external structural factors would not produce any noticeable change in the country's foreign policy behavior. The legacy of World War II produced a lasting "shift in the principal dimension of German power away from military to economic, the eradication of German militarism."[15] Essentially the continuity thesis suggests a true transformation of German foreign policy thought and behavior, portraying Germany as a reformed state, which one proponent of the thesis even considered to be the world's first "post-national state."[16]

The continuity thesis derives its merit from the fact that German foreign policy initially did appear to remain fairly restrained following reunification. It is also correct in pointing to German political culture, as well as national identity, as factors that influence foreign policy behavior. To argue, however, that Germany is forever transformed and that no change has taken place at all since 1990 is just as wrong as predicting a return to pre-Cold War behavior.

As an alternative, I propose an approach that allows for both: continuity in German foreign policy as a result of the influence of historical memory, but also change as a result of the pressures of a changed external environment. I will show that, following the end of the Cold War, Germans were faced with the difficult task of reconciling the lessons of history – which had become such an important part of national identity – with the demands of a post-Cold War system in which Germany did not have the luxury of hiding under the security umbrella the United States had provided for decades. While the former prescribed continuity in the form of a foreign policy that is guided by the principles of antimilitarism, multilateralism, reliability, and responsibility, the latter suddenly called for a more assertive German foreign and security policy that could not always avoid the use of military force or satisfy the strict definitions of multilateralism. In order to remain functional despite the pull in two different directions, a compromise had to be reached. In the end, a slow, but steady re-interpretation of historical memory – and with it the meaning of the lessons of history – occurred.

At the same time, change can only ever be incremental in nature. While the specific meaning of the lessons of history may be subject to re-interpretation and policies may change as a result thereof, foreign policies can not be created *de novo*, but should rather be expected to follow established patterns. In other words, we should expect path dependent policies, which are only changing slowly.

It is important to understand that this approach rests on the assumption that all the elements that contribute to a country's foreign policy behavior are at least partly socially constructed. I argue that foreign policy behavior is best understood as the result of a complex relationship between the way a country's decision makers think and talk about issues (the Thought-Talk-Action Model). Especially in a democratic setting, policy is usually the result of lengthy debates ("talk") in which politicians present competing positions and interpretations ("thought") that advance different preferred policy options. Only the most convincing frames will create consensus and mobilize alliances that support a particular decision ("action"). In the case of Germany, the many coalition governments produced by a proportional electoral system make political debates even more relevant. Think, for instance, about the coalition between the Social Democrats and the Green Party between 1998 and 2005, which frequently created the need for Chancellor Schröder to actively "sell" a policy that might not otherwise have met the approval of the Greens.

In this model, I assume that we cannot treat a country's foreign policy thought as exogenous. We should not expect policy makers across countries – or even within countries – to hold the same views of the world, to interpret events in the same way, or to have the same interests. Human cognition tends to be much more complex than a mere calculation of cost-benefit and expected utility. Actors, therefore, are not always rational, as many traditional approaches assume, but should rather be considered cognitive actors,[17] with all the implications this has for the decision making process. Foreign policy cognition in particular "is 'thick' with cultural memory, emotion, and morality, and state action requires skillful negotiations that build agreement among diverse constituencies."[18] In the case of Germany, historical memory in general, and the lessons of history in particular, should be considered cognitive factors that shape decision makers' thoughts on foreign policy and military intervention, as will be illustrated in more detail below.

Political discourse becomes an important explanatory variable in this model, because it can show how policy makers collectively "think" about certain issues, how they form interests and decide appropriate policies, and therefore helps explain why they act the way they do. Such a discursive approach can be considered a "transmission belt" by which international impulses are translated into policy. Even if one assumes that political talk is "cheap," the question remains why politicians talk the way they do. A possible answer is that they conform to audience expectations, which means that even if the politicians themselves do not genuinely believe what they say, they believe that someone wants to hear it, thus expressing what is important to society as a whole.

Talk mediates between thought and action, especially in a group setting – as all democratic decision making processes tend to be – where talk becomes indispensable as a tool for forming a consensus among the individual policy makers, but also as a means for them to justify their decisions to a larger audience. Policy makers "are forced to give reasons (verbal or written) for the way they act in politically binding contexts."[19] Words therefore do not only reflect thought and action, but also have the power to mold them.

Ultimately, action is the result of both thought and talk, as outlined above.

German Foreign Policy Thought: National Interests vs. National Identity

In further examining the element of foreign policy thought, I assume that both national interests and national identity play an important role in a country's decision making process, and furthermore, that both should be thought of as "ideas" that are – at least partly – socially constructed.[20] In the case of Germany, the experience of World War II, and how that experience is remembered, has largely shaped the interpretation of German national interests and how they are to be pursued, as well as the interpretation of German national identity.

The idea of "historical memory" as part of a country's collective memory is generally ascribed to Maurice Halbwachs. He defined it as the embodiment of collective experiences that "is stored and interpreted by social institutions."[21] As such, historical memory is shared even by generations who have not lived through the initial or formative experiences. Halbwachs suggests that these effects can last up to 100 years after the event that comes to dominate collective memory. The past, it would appear, is ever present in political decision making; it is, perhaps, even more important than present demands and external factors.

Not surprisingly, especially traumatic experiences shape a country's identity and its politics more than any others and have a tendency to remain part of the collective consciousness for several generations. Robert Jervis once wrote that "the only thing as important for a nation as its revolution is its last major war."[22] Even though he allows for a certain generational effect to take place over time, he also believes that the "lessons of history can become institutionalized in textbooks, rules, and even language itself."[23] Examples of such institutionalization of memory in Germany are plenty, ranging from the moral judgment of German actions in history textbooks, to the provisions in the Basic Law regulating the use of force, to the law against *Volksverhetzung* (incitement of the masses) and denying the Holocaust, all the way to the continued insistence on Conscription as a means to firmly anchor the military within German society, even though the practice is becoming increasingly irrational and costly.

In Germany, the last war tends to overwhelm any other aspects of German history that may potentially have come to shape German politics. The reason for that is quite simple: the experiences under the Nazi regime, the utter defeat and occupation in 1945, combined with the intense re-education measures initiated by the Allies have produced a collective memory in which there is little room anything else. "[A]ll discussion of German history seems to begin and end with the Nazis."[24] Because the experience of World War II has been elevated to such heights in the minds of the German people, and because Germans are more conscious of their own history than most other people, historical memory is perhaps disproportionately powerful in shaping present foreign policy.[25]

One might think of historical memory as a collectively shared frame of reference for behavior. The more unfamiliar a situation is to decision makers, the more important the lessons of history are for providing a type of "compass." It is easy to see how the unfamiliarity of the post-

Cold War environment at least initially caused German politicians to hold on to historical traditions.

In addition to the notion of historical memory, path dependency is another useful concept in describing the continued prominence of history in German foreign policy. Although the literature on path dependency is mostly concerned with the constraining effects of early choices in economics, it does seem possible to apply some of the same argument to political science. The idea is that "choices formed when an institution is being formed or when a policy is being formulated have a constraining effect into the future." [26] Because that is the case, one cannot completely understand present choices without knowing the historical path that has led decision makers to this junction. "To capture the critical moments and actions of the particular case also requires an understanding of the constraints that derive from past actions."[27]

Path dependency does not simply mean that "history matters." While that is true, it also trivializes the issue and does not provide a focused enough explanation of the causal mechanisms at work. Perhaps a better way to think of this is in terms of Margaret Levi's tree metaphor: from the same trunk, there are many different branches and smaller branches one might follow when climbing a tree. Although it is possible to go back or to even jump from one branch to another, it is more likely that one will follow the branch one chose in the beginning (unless, of course, that branch dies).[28]

Levi justifies her arguments in terms of rational choice, saying that once a path is chosen, it often becomes too costly to turn around, as "the entrenchment of certain institutional arrangements obstruct an easy reversal of the initial choice." In the case of Germany, whose main priority following the disaster of World War II was rehabilitation, a sudden reversal in direction or even "jumping off the tree" would have potentially devastating consequences for German credibility. The rest of the world, and certainly Europe in particular, still keep a wary eye on German behavior, perhaps half-expecting a return to the aggressive militarism that many still seem to associate with Germany. German leaders are very much aware of this and have always tried to remain as transparent and inconspicuous as possible in their foreign policy rhetoric and behavior. As a result, the notion of path dependency makes complete sense, both from a cultural and from a rational point of view.

Critics might argue that this theory is flawed, because it does not allow for change to happen. If history really is so important, how does change in a country's behavior occur? If, for instance, the experience of World War II is such a formative one in German foreign policy thought and behavior, and if it indeed has become institutionalized, should we not expect the same thought and behavior to continue indefinitely?

This criticism is valid, if one treats historical memory as fixed, making it too deterministic by far. Although the past is undeniably constraining current German foreign policy, it would be utopian to assume that this will be the case forever. Instead, historical memory – as well as national identity and national interests – should be treated as discourses rather than fixed variables. Because historical memory is discursive in nature, it can very well change, although there are definite limits to how much and how quickly it can do so. Not just any alternative interpretation of the past is possible once a dominant narrative has developed. In Germany, for instance, the dominant narrative of historical memory has been so inextricably linked to the concepts of *Wiedergutmachung* (atonement), *Verantwortungspolitik* (responsible politics), and a complete rejection of aggressive militarism and fascist ideology for so long, that it simply is not possible to adopt a new dominant narrative that is too far removed from the current narrative without great costs to Germany's credibility in Europe and the world. Instead, any change has to be incremental.

Certain aspects of a county's historical memory are perhaps more open to reinterpretation than others, depending on how deeply they have been internalized by society. Germans pride themselves on having learned the lessons of history and therefore being unlikely to repeat past mistakes. That is the single most important element of German historical memory. Derived from that are the general lessons Germany learned from the experience of World War II: responsibility, reliability, multilateralism, predictability, and antimilitarism. All of these have become intrinsic components of Germany's self-understanding as a history-conscious nation and have impacted every aspect of German life, though none more than the practice of foreign policy.

I argue that at this point in time, these general lessons – with the exception of strict antimilitarism, which will be explained later – are currently not open for reinterpretation as they are too intrinsically linked to German national identity. So what do Germans do when they find themselves in an international environment that consistently challenges these lessons? Well, the general lessons might not be open for debate, but the specific meaning of these lessons are. Most of them are fairly abstract in the first place and therefore potentially open to interpretation, if the need should arise. For instance, "responsibility" could be defined in a number of ways. The general lesson of needing to practice a "responsible" foreign policy can remain intact, while the specific interpretation of what it means to be responsible can change.

In the end, change depends on the existence of pressure upon the dominant discourse. I argue that during the Cold War, the dominant narratives were mostly unchallenged, because there was no external pressure upon Germans to reconsider these lessons. This explains why following the end of the Cold War and German reunification no immediate reinterpretation of the dominant discourse on historical memory occurred, resulting in continuity of German politics rather than change. When the pressure from the new international environment increased over the years a reinterpretation of historical memory finally became unavoidable.

Despite the importance of historical memory, it is utopian to think that this prevents German politicians from placing the pursuit of national interests at the top of their foreign policy agenda. According to my model, national interests and historical memory both shape foreign policy thought as well as each other. Both are at least partly socially constructed and should therefore not be treated as given. To claim that all states have the same interests, as positivist theories of international relations tend to do, does not do justice to the complexity of political realities. A country does not pursue interests because of exogenous factors, such as its geography or its power position in the international system, alone; it is just as important to examine how the national interest is defined in public and elite discourse, and how it may be constrained by historical memory.

Interestingly, German politicians are notoriously reluctant to talk about national interests. Throughout the Cold War and during most of the 1990s, German foreign policy was justified mostly in terms of responsibility, the lessons of history, and humanitarian interests, as opposed to national interests. Germans almost seemed afraid to even hint at an interest-based foreign policy.[29] This is a direct result of the experience of World War II, which still looms over policy makers' heads. Talk about German interests is invariably linked to past ambitions, making it nearly impossible to talk about them without resurrecting the ghosts (and fears) of the past. That is why a German Chancellor, if (s)he speaks of interests at all, "needs to explain matters that other leaders do not need to explain: what is a legitimate German national interest abroad? When should German forces become engaged abroad?"[30]

The legacy of World War II has significantly shaped the kinds of interests German leaders feel they are allowed to pursue, where they can pursue them, and the manner in which they can pursue them. With regard to the former, it is undeniable that Germany's foreign policy ambitions have been curtailed as a result of the war. The mere thought of territorial expansion – the *Drang nach Osten* (the urge to expand eastward), which had so long dominated German foreign policy – was taboo in postwar Germany, as was the use of military force. During the last sixty years, foreign policy makers have preferred to keep a low profile beyond the immediate defense of national and alliance territory, wishing above all to go largely unnoticed. Germany at its most ambitious has striven to be a *Mitführungsmacht* (co-leading power), rather than a *Führungsmacht* (leading power).

The question of where Germany can pursue its interests was until recently very limited: Any area in which soldiers of the Wehrmacht had been engaged during World War II remained off-limits, no matter the situation. When the international community was discussing a peacekeeping operation in the former Yugoslavia in the mid-1990s, former Chancellor Helmut Kohl refused to consider committing German troops to such an endeavor, arguing that Germany simply could not send its military into a region where German soldiers had committed such atrocities sixty years earlier. Relations with Eastern Europe in general remain affected by the memories of World War II. For instance, no German leader has thus far felt comfortable enough to bring up the matter of the Sudeten Germans, who were expelled from their homes by Czechoslovakia in 1945 and have received neither compensation for their property nor a formal apology (whereas the German government has continuously offered both in large quantities).

The aspect of German national interests that has been affected the most by the legacy of World War II is the means by which they can be pursued. Before 1945, territorial expansion and military force were considered appropriate means to achieving security and influence; after 1945, diplomatic and economic means were all that was left to German leaders, effectively turning Germany into a civilian power.[31] In addition, unilateralism was no longer an option, while predictability and transparency became indispensable.

While its ambitions may have been curbed, Germany's national interests at their most basic level have not changed: as the land of the middle – sharing borders with nine other countries – security and influence continue to be of the utmost importance. Because of its geographic location, Germany has always had to look East and West – and occasionally North and South – in its foreign policy. Unlike the United States and Great Britain, Germany has never had the luxury of retreating into isolationism, but rather had to "play the game of foreign policy" at all times. Even after 1945, the new German leaders almost immediately began to play both sides once again, or at least attempted to keep their options open. Although ultimately the *Westpolitik* (Western politics) took precedence, Germany insisted on having an *Ostpolitik* (Eastern politics) as well throughout the Cold War, often to the dismay of the United States, which feared potential Soviet influences.

Even though Europe has been exceedingly peaceful since the end of World War II, and is well advanced on the road to integration, Germany still cannot help but be aware of the goings-on around it. In fact, one might argue that even though European integration was conceived of as an insurance against German ambitions, it has simultaneously contributed a great deal to alleviating German fears that originated from its vulnerable geographic location. Stability on the continent is very much in Germany's interest, both from a political and from an economical point of view, as is the achievement of as much influence within the European Union as possible.

The end of the Cold War has changed the perception of German interests, because it has turned Germany from a country that was passively benefiting from European security – mainly provided by the United States as a result of its desire to contain the Soviet Union – into one of the guarantors of security on the continent. At least, that is the role that many see for the reunified Germany. Even the staunchest defenders of the German-American friendship and the American-European alliance would have to admit that the end of the Cold War has also reduced America's strategic interest in Europe, which is why the U.S. security umbrella which had been so generously provided for decades can no longer be taken for granted. While it is undeniable that the United States still has some interest in Europe as a strategic location for its military bases, it is equally undeniable that this is not considered to be a matter of American national security any longer. In fact, Donald Rumsfeld's 2003 comments about a potential move of U.S. bases to the "new Europe," following the disagreement between Germany, France, and America over the war against Iraq, have made the point quite clearly.[32] In addition, every post-Cold War U.S. president has repeatedly called for greater burden-sharing and for greater European responsibility in areas that are considered to be Europe's problem. As one of the largest and richest countries in the European Union, Germany is naturally expected to take on a leadership role.

In short, the post-Cold War environment has effectively put pressure on the definition of German national interest, and is challenging some of the lessons of history that have become part of the country's national identity, which Germans have held so dearly for decades. In particular, Germany's preference for strict antimilitarism is not feasible any longer, given the demands placed on its foreign policy by the changed external environment. During the Cold War, the lessons of history were largely commensurable with the external environment; interests and identity were largely commensurable, as they were both based on the same goal: to allow German rehabilitation and a return to the international community as a fully sovereign and unified state. Other interests were either prohibited or, as in the case of German security, were largely taken care of by others.

German Foreign Policy Talk:
The Social Construction of Discourse

> *We should not ask what the words mean,*
> *as though they contained secrets,*
> *but what they are doing,*
> *as though they embodied actions.*[33]

As outlined above, the elements of foreign policy thought – historical memory and national interest – are considered to be largely socially constructed. It follows that scholars of foreign policy decision making should pay close attention to political discourse as the means by which the meanings of these elements are negotiated and re-negotiated. Such an approach, of course, is derived from the fundamental assumption that humans use language to inscribe meaning into the world. "[D]iscursive phenomena [are] more than reflections of knowledge and power; as manifestations of society's ongoing activity of asserting its identity, its discourses serve a constitutive function."[34] It is through discourse that humans define their reality and themselves.

Indeed, there is an "increasingly accepted equation between 'discursive practices' and political practices" [35] as well. Because "political problems are socially constructed, whether or not a situation is perceived as a political problem depends on the narrative in which it is discussed."[36] Politicians in their talk construct a vision of the world which can constitute identity, structure deliberation, and constrain action.[37]

Political discourse becomes especially important in democratic decision making settings. Given the likelihood of competing positions and interpretations in any political debate involving a great number of decision makers, one might think of discourse as a means for creating consensus and for mobilizing coalitions, for establishing a common position which ultimately becomes the basis for action.

Finally, discourse can reconcile realities with incommensurable beliefs and values.[38] In the German case, discourse helps to reconcile the lessons of history with the demands of the new political reality the end of the Cold War has created.

Foreign Policy Action: Military Interventions

In theory, the model put forth here could be used to analyze any type of foreign policy action. In this book, however, I am exclusively interested in military intervention for two reasons: the question of military interventions is the single most sensitive foreign policy topic in Germany, and it is the area that has been affected the most by the legacy of World War II. In order to understand the significance of historical memory for Germany's ability to participate in such military operations abroad, I examine the three most recent cases in which Germans were called upon to do so: (1) the NATO-led airstrikes in Kosovo in 1999, in which Germany actively participated; (2) the U.S.-led invasion of Afghanistan in 2001, in which Germany also participated, though much more hesitantly than in Kosovo; (3) the war against Iraq in 2003, in which Germany refused to participate.

In the years between the end of the Cold War and the Kosovo intervention, German behavior with regard to military interventions had been characterized more by continuity than change. Table 1.1 summarizes Germany's participation in military operations between 1987 and 1998, showing that although there has been an increase in both the quality and quantity of German contributions, one can certainly not call German foreign policy during that time period aggressive or even a return to normalcy. In 1987, Germany's culture of reticence was challenged directly for the first time since 1945[39] when the United States requested military assistance from its European allies following a few skirmishes with Iran in the Persian Gulf. The German government was asked to contribute several ships for the protection of Kuwaiti oil tankers, but denied the request on the basis of constitutional restrictions. Instead, decision makers approved the deployment of a number of ships to the Mediterranean, as long as they remained within NATO territory. In 1989, Germany contributed to an international police force in Namibia under the auspices of the United Nations, but support was limited to non-combat units.

In 1987, Germany's culture of reticence was challenged directly for the first time since 1945[40] when the United States requested military assistance from its European allies following a few skirmishes with Iran in the Persian Gulf. The German government was asked to contribute several ships for the protection of Kuwaiti oil tankers, but denied the request on the basis of constitutional restrictions. Instead, decision makers

Table 1.1: German Military Participation between 1987 and 1998

	Conflict/Military Operation	Scope of German Participation
1987	Persian Gulf, Escort of Kuwaiti ships; US skirmishes with Iran; mine sweeping	Logistical support only; German ships to Mediterranean, but not to Gulf region
1989	Namibia Peacekeeping operation (UNTAG)	Contribution to international police force
1990-1991	Gulf War	Financial and logistical support only; dispatch of 200 soldiers and 18 fighter jets to Turkey as part of a NATO contingent
1992	Cambodia, Peacekeeping operation (UNAMIC)	Medical troops
1991-1996	Adriatic, Monitoring of embargo against FRY (Operation Sharp Guard)	Naval forces ("no combat operation")
1993-1994	Somalia (UNOSOM II)	Supply and transport units
1993-1995	Bosnia-Herzegovina (UNPROFOR)	Logistical support only (airlifts to Sarajevo)
1993-1995	Bosnia-Herzegovina, Monitoring of no-fly zone; NATO airstrikes against FRY	Airforce personnel as part of AWACS unit; no participation in NATO airstrikes
1994	Georgia (UNOMIG)	10 German medical officers and military observers as part of UN peacekeeping force
1995-1996	Bosnia-Herzegovina (IFOR)	Some 3,000 non-combat ground troops, stationed in Croatia
1996	Bosnia-Herzegovina (SFOR)	Some 3,000 ground troops (including combat troops), stationed in Bosnia-Herzegovina
1998	Iraq, US-led air raids	Offer to grant US the use of military bases in Germany; no participation in attacks

Source: Baumann and Hellmann (2001).

makers approved the deployment of a number of ships to the Mediterranean, as long as they remained within NATO territory. In 1989, Germany contributed to an international police force in Namibia under the auspices of the United Nations, but support was limited to non-combat units.

After reunification, many expected a significant change in Germany's attitude toward participation in international military operations. The first test came quickly in the form of the United States' request for military assistance in the 1991 war against Iraq. German decision makers – highly unprepared for this challenge, both materially and emotionally – denied that request, pointing once again to the German constitution, which contained a clause against the use of the German military in out-of-area missions. Although some representatives of the Christian Democrats (CDU) declared that it was time to move past antimilitarism, the German government (also run by the CDU) limited its support to what had come to be known as "checkbook diplomacy:" Contributing more than $12 billion to the war, but not sending any troops. In addition, Germany provided logistical support and dispatched 18 fighter jets to Turkey as part of a NATO contingent. Back home, public opinion was highly critical of the war effort, leading to numerous demonstrations under the motto "No blood for oil!" It was mainly public opinion that prevented policy makers from sending even a token force to appease the United States and to ward off accusations of free-riding.

Between 1992 and 1996, Germany participated in several United Nations missions, but continued its policy of not deploying combat troops. In 1991-92, German medical personnel assisted United Nations peacekeeping troops in Cambodia. Between 1992 and 1996, German naval forces took part in the monitoring of an embargo against Yugoslavia in the Adriatic. The government took special care to declare that this was not a combat operation. In Somalia in 1993-94, German supply and transport units joined the United Nations troops of UNOSOM II.

In 1994, the German Constitutional Court ruled that nothing in the Basic Law prohibited the deployment of German combat troops in out-of-area missions. From a legal point of view, all obstacles to an active German military participation abroad had been removed with this ruling. However, German leaders continued to approve only non-combat missions, such as the deployment of 10 (!) medical officers and military observers as part of a United Nations peacekeeping force in Georgia. Between 1993 and 1995, Germans offered logistical support for United Nations troops in Bosnia-Herzegovina as part of UNPROFOR, and deployed air-force personnel for the monitoring of a no-fly zone in the same area. There was no German participation in the NATO airstrikes against Yugoslavia.

The first serious commitment to a military mission abroad after reunification came in the form of 3,000 German troops deployed as part of the NATO-led force policing the Dayton Peace Accords of 1995 in the Balkans (IFOR). The German contingent consisted mainly of logistical and transport units, and was stationed in Croatia, well away from the actual problem zone. Nevertheless, this mission represented a major step on the way to a more engaged foreign policy. Only a year later, the German government approved the deployment of combat troops for the first time in connection with the IFOR follow-up mission SFOR. These troops were regularly stationed in Bosnia-Herzegovina. It seemed as though this operation would herald a new era in German foreign policy making. Six years after reunification, Germans finally seemed to have shed their reluctance to use military force. Despite this progress, however, it soon became clear that Germany still had a long way to go before it could be considered a "normal" nation. In 1998, the government granted the United States the use of some of its military bases for the U.S.-led air raids against Iraq, but once again refused to participate actively.

German military participation abroad certainly increased between 1987 and 1998. However, it would be exaggerated to speak of an extremely active, or even aggressive, foreign policy. In most cases, German involvement was restricted to logistical and medical support, and virtually all such decisions were accompanied by heated political debates about the morality of the mission. Overall, the time period preceding the first case analyzed in this book was characterized more by continuity than change.

Research Methodology:
Taking a Linguistic Approach to Decision Making

As outlined above, my theoretical model is based on the assumption that political discourse is an important explanatory variable for a country's foreign policy behavior, which is why I have adopted discourse analysis as my primary method of inquiry. Political debates "leave a long trail of communication," a "detailed conversational map that reveals important dimensions of political reasoning that often goes unnoticed by traditional analysis.[41] I have drawn such a conversational map – or a rhetorical map – that offers insights into the kind of reasoning German politicians employ when they talk about foreign policy and the use of military force, and how their way of talking is connected to the outcome of the decision making process.

My data consists of transcripts of Bundestag debates. The Bundestag is the lower chamber of the German parliament and is the locus of foreign policy decision making. For each case – Kosovo, Afghanistan, and Iraq – I monitored all Bundestag debates for approximately eight months before and four months after each event, but only included those debates that actually address the issue in my analysis.

For Kosovo, I selected a total of eight debates, beginning on October 16th, 1998, and ending on May 7th, 1999. For Afghanistan, I selected eight debates as well, beginning on September 12th, 2001, and ending on December 19th, 2001. For Iraq, I chose three debates, taking place in February and March of 2003.

Organization of the Book

The next chapter, Chapter 2, presents a case study of the Bundestag debates that accompanied the German decision to participate in the NATO-led airstrikes against the Serbs in Kosovo in 1999. Chapter 3 analyzes the second empirical case, the debates leading up to the German participation in the U.S.-led intervention in Afghanistan in 2001. Chapter 4 examines the debates that accompanied Germany's decision not to participate in the war against Iraq in 2003. Finally, the concluding chapter (5) presents a summary of the findings, a comparison across the three cases, and implications for the future of German foreign policy in the 21st century, especially as regards the role of historical memory as an influential variable in the decision making process.

---

[1] Quoted in: Heneghan, Tom (2000). *Unchained Eagle: Germany after the Wall.* Financial Times Prentice Hall, p.7.

[2] Kulish, Nicholas (2008). "Germany Confronts Holocaust Legacy Anew," *New York Times*, January 29 2008.

[3] This phrase is part of a quote by historian Ernst Nolte about Germany's obsession with the past: "Between Myth and Revisionism? The Third Reich in the Perspective of the 1980s," in: Erich Nolte and Michael Stürmer (1987), eds., *Historikerstreit.* Munich: Piper.

[4] Richard J. Evans (1999). *In Defense of History.* New York: W. W. Norton & Company, p. 3.

[5] At least there appears to be the "persistent German perception that the eyes of the world are continuously upon them." Atina Grossmann (2000). "The "Goldhagen Effect:" Memory, Repetition, and Responsibility in the New Germany," in: Geoff Eley, ed., *The "Goldhagen" Effect: History, Memory,*

Nazism – Facing the German Past. Ann Arbor, MI: University of Michigan Press, p. 110.

[6] Reunification added five new states to Germany's territory, which amounted to a 33% increase; its population went from around 60 million people – comparable to France and Britain – to over 80 million; simultaneously, Germany's economic and military strength increased significantly as well. Cf. Volker Rittberger, ed., (2000). *German Foreign Policy since Unification: Theories and Case Studies.* Manchester, UK: Manchester University Press, p. 58-61.

[7] See Michael Staack (2000). *Handelsstaat Deutschland: Deutsche Außenpolitik in einem neuen internationalen System.* Paderborn, Germany: Schöning, p. 23; and Gunther Hellmann (1998). "Die prekäre Macht: Deutschland an der Schwelle zum 21. Jahrhundert," in: Wolf-Dieter Eberwein und Karl Kaiser, eds., *Deutschlands neue Außenpolitik, Vol. 4: Institutionen und Ressourcen.* Munich: Oldenbourg, p. 256.

[8] Stephen Peter Rosen (1995). "Military Effectiveness: Why Society Matters," *International Security,* Vol. 19, No. 4 (Spring), p. 5.

[9] Matthias Zimmer (1997). *Germany: Phoenix in Trouble?* Edmonton, Alberta, Canada: University of Alberta Press; Thomas F. Banchoff (1999). *The German Problem Transformed: Institutions, Politics, and Foreign Policy, 1945-1995.* Ann Arbor, MI: University of Michigan Press.

[10] John Mearsheimer (1990). "Back to the Future: Instability in Europe after the Cold War," *International Affairs,* Vol. 15, No. 1 (Summer), pp. 5-56.

[11] Zimmer (1997); John G. Ikenberry, ed., (2002). *America Unrivaled: The Future of the Balance of Power.* Ithaca, NY: Cornell University Press.

[12] John S. Duffield (1998). World Power Forsaken: Political Culture, International Institutions, and German Security Policy after Unification. Stanford, CA: Stanford University Press; Roberta Haar (2001). Nation States as Schizophrenics: Germany and Japan as Post-Cold War Actors. Westport, CT: Praeger; Michael Stürmer (1992). Die Grenzen der Macht. Berlin: Siedler Verlag, p. 247.

[13] Peter J. Katzenstein, (1997). *Tamed Power: Germany in Europe.* Ithaca, NY: Cornell University Press, p. 8.

[14] Thomas U. Berger (1998). *Cultures of Antimilitarism: National Security in Germany and Japan.* Baltimore, MD: Johns Hopkins University Press, p. 167.

[15] Thomas F. Banchoff (1999). The German Problem Transformed: Institutions, Politics, and Foreign Policy, 1945-1995. Ann Arbor, MI: University of Michigan Press, p. 43.

[16] Anthony Glees (1996). Reinventing Germany: German Political Development since 1945. Dulles, VA: Berg.

[17] See Jerel A. Rosati (2001). "The Power of Human Cognition in the Study of World Politics," *International Studies Review,* Vol. 2, No. 3 (Autumn), pp. 45-75.

[18] Francis A. Beer and Robert Hariman, eds., (1996). *Post-Realism: The Rhetorical Turn in International Relations.* East Lansing, MI: Michigan State University Press, p. 19.

[19] Henrik Larsen (1997). *Foreign Policy and Discourse Analysis.* New York, NY: Routledge, p. 13.

[20] cf. Alexander Wendt (1999). *Social Theory of International Politics*. New York, NY: Cambridge University Press.

[21] Maurice Halbwachs (1992). *On Collective Memory*, trans., ed., and intro. Lewis A. Coser, Chicago, IL: University of Chicago Press, p. 24.

[22] Robert Jervis (1976). *Perception and Misperception in International Politics*. Princeton, NJ: Princeton University Press, p. 266.

[23] ibid., p. 267.

[24] Steven Ozment (2004). *A Mighty Fortress: A New History of the German People*. New York, NY: Harper Collins, p. 6.

[25] Yacoov Vertzberger argued that "the importance of historical heritage in shaping cognition and perception increases in proportion to the historical consciousness of a society" (in: ibid. 1990. *The World in Their Minds*, pp. 265-266.)

[26] Ian Greener (2005). "The Potential of Path Dependence in Political Studies," *Politics*, vol. 25, no. 1, pp. 62-72, at p. 62; see also Hall and Taylor (1996), Koelble (1995), and Peters (2001).

[27] Margaret Levi (1997). "A Model, a Method, and a Map: Rational Choice in Comparative and Historical Analysis," in: Mark I. Lichbach and Alan S. Zuckerman, eds., *Comparative Politics; Rationality, Culture, and Structure*. Cambridge, UK: Cambridge University Press, pp. 19-42, at p. 28.

[28] ibid.

[29] To be sure, this pertains mostly to the realm of security and defense policy. In the realm of economics, German leaders have generally been much less self-conscious in talking about German interests and in pursuing them aggressively.

[30] W. R. Smyser (1999). *From Yalta to Berlin*, p. 415.

[31] Cf. Sebastian Harnisch and Hanns M. Maull (2001). *Germany as a Civilian Power? The Foreign Policy of the Berlin Republic*. New York, NY: Palgrave.

[32] See Ian Fischer (2003). "U.S. Eyes a Willing Romania As a New Comrade in Arms," *New York Times*, July 16th, 2003.

[33] Denis Donoghue, *The Sovereign Ghost: Studies in Imagination*. Berkeley, CA: University of California Press. p. 54.

[34] Gerard Hauser (1999). *Vernacular Voices*. Upper Saddle River, NJ: Pearson Prentice Hall, p. 113.

[35] Corcoran (1990). "Language and Politics," in: David L. Swanson and Dan Nimmo, New Directions in Political Communication: A Resource Book; Cameron (1985); Edelman (1988); Thomas Diez (1999) Die EU lesen: Diskursive Knotenpunkte in der britischen Europadebatte, Opladen: Leske & Budrich; Jacob Torfing (1999) New theories of discourse: Laclau, Mouffe and Žižek, Oxford: Blackwell;

[36] Maarten A. Hajer, "Discourse coalitions and the Institutionalisation of Practice. The case of acid rain in Britain," in: J. Forester and F. Fischer, eds., The Argumentative Turn in Policy and Planning, Durham, NC: Duke University Press, p. 44

[37] Francis A. Beer and Robert Hariman, eds., (1996). *Post-Realism: The Rhetorical Turn in International Relations*. East Lansing, MI: Michigan State University Press, p. 24.

[38] Gerard Hauser (1999). *Vernacular Voices*, p. 19.

---

[39] Between the years of 1945 and 1987, not a single German soldier was deployed in a combat mission.

[40] Between the years of 1945 and 1987, not a single German soldier was deployed in a combat mission.

[41] Francis A. Beer and Robert Hariman, eds., (1996), p. 371.

2
Has Germany Crossed the Rubicon?
The Case of NATO and Kosovo

"Negotiations without weapons are like music without instruments."
– Frederick the Great (1740-1786)

On March 24th, 1999, fourteen German Tornadoes took off from their base in order to participate in the NATO-led military intervention "Allied Force." For 78 consecutive days, allied planes bombed Serbian targets with the goal to force Slobodan Milošević to sign the Treaty of Rambouillet, which would provide an interim solution for the war-torn Kosovo region.

For many observers in Germany and abroad this event marked a drastic break with Germany's postwar foreign policy, as it was the first time since 1945 that German troops engaged in an offensive combat operation. Even more surprisingly, this step was taken without a United Nations mandate, in a region that lies outside of NATO's area of responsibility. Not only that, but it was a Red-Green[1] government – newly elected and inaugurated in October of 1998 – that sanctioned the Bundeswehr's deployment. For years, both parties – though the Greens in particular – had been known for their decidedly pacifist orientations. For a Red-Green coalition to preside over the first combat mission in the history of the Federal Republic raises important questions about the future of German foreign policy and the continuation of its culture of antimilitarism.

The political and intellectual debate that accompanied the airstrikes was as controversial as could be expected. The nature of commentaries ranged from those that welcomed a more assertive German foreign policy[2] to those that claimed to recognize the first signs of a resurfacing of aggressive German nationalism, *Machtpolitik*, and possibly even a new form of *Drang nach Osten.*[3] Most commentators, however, appeared to be mostly perplexed at this sudden transformation. After all, the same arguments that were now used to justify the Kosovo mission – mainly having to do with Germany's lessons of history – had been cited by the German Bundestag when it refused to participate in the mission in Bosnia during the early 1990s.[4] This development begs the question of whether Germany has finally thrown off the shackles of its World

War II legacy. And if so, whether this step has occurred for better or worse?

From Negotiations to Airstrikes

Germany had first shown its commitment to solving the conflict in the Kosovo region in 1997. The Serbs, who considered Kosovo to be part of Greater Serbia, had consistently increased their military presence in the region and begun to engage in acts of murder and expulsion against the Kosovar-Albanians. Germany was then part of the Contact Group, an informal grouping of influential countries with an interest in the Balkans; other members included the United States, the United Kingdom, France, Italy, and Russia. Germany in particular pushed for greater diplomatic efforts to reduce the tension in the region and to force Milošević to withdraw his forces. When neither sanctions against Belgrade nor diplomatic efforts convinced the Serb leader, NATO threatened the use of force.

Unfortunately, the threats initially proved to be harmless as NATO did not appear willing to carry them out. Instead, the organization let itself be engaged in drawn-out negotiations with Milošević, the only success of which was the permission to send an unarmed OSCE observer force into Kosovo. Meanwhile, members of NATO continued to lobby for support of a military operation. The outgoing CDU-FDP Government pledged to make a contribution, should it become necessary, in 1998, and the newly elected SPD-Greens coalition government reaffirmed the pledge on October 16th, 1998, after it had assumed office.

The final straw came in the form of the discovery of a massacre of Albanian villagers in Račak, carried out by Serbian forces. The event represented a critical turning point in the situation, as it resulted in renewed threats of bombing by NATO and – perhaps more importantly – the dawning realization that Milošević had never had any intention to cooperate, but had merely been appeasing the alliance.

Perhaps the fact that NATO's fiftieth anniversary was just around the corner added to the determination to resolve the conflict once and for all, as continued inactivity, especially in light of the ultimatum given to Milošević more than a year prior, could be construed as a sign of NATO's incapability and thus jeopardized its credibility. In the context of the organization's so-called "crisis of identity" following the end of the Cold War, the situation in Kosovo was perceived as critical, because it was a chance to prove NATO's worth and to make a case for its continued existence as a regional security and peacekeeping force.

The Rambouillet talks, held between February 6th and February 23rd of 1999, represented the last attempt to solve the crisis at the conference table. The Kosovar-Albanians showed their good-will by agreeing to accept Kosovo's status as autonomous rather than fully independent, but the Serbs refused the compromise. The Rambouillet talks were broken off without an agreement, and NATO finally carried out its threat on March 24th, 1999.

German Historical Memory of the Balkans: Past and Present

Former Yugoslavia represents a highly sensitive area for German foreign policy. The legacy of World War II requires a significant amount of tact and historical understanding from German politicians dealing with the region. Up until the mid-1990s, the mere thought of once again sending even German peacekeeping troops into the Balkans was absolutely taboo. Nonetheless, that very need arose in November of 1995, following the Dayton Peace Accords. The request for 4,000 German troops as part of the United Nations' Implementation Force (IFOR) set off a fundamental debate about the legacy of World War II and the nature of German foreign policy henceforth.

The Dayton Debates represented the first step toward a narrative of normalization in Germany's historical memory with regard to this particular region. While only a few years prior former Chancellor Helmut Kohl had adamantly refused to send German troops into the Balkans, a region where he said German soldiers had committed the most heinous atrocities,[5] the dominant interpretation during the Dayton Debates focused on a very different interpretation of historical memory.

The debates did not seek to erase the memory of the past in order to free foreign policy from the constraints of historical memory. On the contrary: the past was ever present in the political debates. Many of the speakers acknowledged openly that fifty years earlier Germans under Hitler had used "armed force … for the oppression of people."[6] They also admitted that "German soldiers [had] been misused in the past by a criminal regime to break international law and destroy peace."[7] Nonetheless, the exact nature of German historical memory had begun to change. The previous interpretations of memory had accepted absolute blame for atrocities committed by Germans and perceived it as an insurmountable obstacle to the use of German military force in the region. Now the same events were interpreted as being the fault perhaps not so much of the German people/soldiers, but that of a "criminal regime" that "misused" its soldiers.

Such phrases suggest a shifting of the blame from the German people – even the soldiers of the Wehrmacht – to the German regime at the time. "German soldiers were forced in the past to break the law."[8] By doing so, the members of the Bundestag created a version of historical memory that would allow German participation in the IFOR mission. After all, if the German people did not willingly commit the crimes in the Balkans out of spite or deep-seated prejudice, but as a result of being forced by an oppressive regime, then it follows that under a different, democratic regime, there should be no apprehensions about the deployment of German soldiers into the region.

Not only did this interpretation of historical memory allow German military participation, it mandated it. "We are all very much aware that Germany was liberated. ... This results in the right and the duty to liberate others or to bring freedom to others."[9] After the Allies risked the lives of their soldiers in order to liberate Germany from the Nazis, it now fell to Germany to do the same for others. The very same history that prevented the use of force in 1991-93 now required it. "[H]ere acts a different Germany, a Germany which has learned from its history,"[10] a country that has become "adult enough [to] enter into fully natural international obligations."[11]

From such interpretations of historical memory followed a moral imperative, a special responsibility as a democratic state that has learned the lessons of its history and that obeys the rule of law, to right the wrongs committed under Hitler and to "give a country a spark of hope with the help of German soldiers, where once before German soldiers brought no hope."[12]

In the end, the Bundestag authorized the deployment of 4,000 troops as part of the United Nations' Implementation Force (IFOR), as well as for the successor mission Stabilization Force (SFOR). Although neither mission required the active use of force, they represent a milestone in Germany's post-Cold War foreign policy. One might even think of Bosnia as having "provided the learning ground"[13] for Kosovo, as well as having paved the way for an even more significant reinterpretation of historical memory with regard to the Balkan region.

In part, the same arguments laid out above apply to the case of Kosovo: the memory of the past no longer prevents the deployment of German troops into the region. In addition, the generally friendly welcome of German IFOR peacekeepers by the Bosnian population went a long way to erase the negative image of German soldiers and to reduce any lingering tensions and animosities.[14] All in all, Germany's first experience back in the Balkans after almost fifty years was considered to be a success.

An important aspect of German historical memory that likely played a role in the foreign policy thinking of German leaders when faced with the situation in Kosovo a few years later is the Serbs' claim that Kosovo was part of a "Greater Serbia." Germans are no strangers to such sweeping territorial claims. For many years the desire to realize the ideal of a "Greater Germany" (*Großdeutschland*) dominated German foreign policy. When the National Assembly convened in St. Paul's Church in Frankfurt in 1948-49 to adopt a constitution and to elect a national government, the question of what regions would be part of the new Germany first arose.[15] One of the offered solutions was that of a Greater Germany, which would consist of all German regions including Austria, Bohemia, and northern Italy, and be headed by a Habsburg emperor.

Great Germany came to be associated with aggressive nationalism, a militarist foreign policy, and a glorified imperial past, all of which are notions that contradict contemporary German thought. The idea of a Greater Germany had been completely discredited in connection with the Zero Hour (*Stunde Null*), the "rebirth" of the German state in 1945. Indeed, any territorial ambitions were now associated with everything the new Germany wanted to distance itself from: Germany's tumultuous unification in the 19th century, the Wilhelmine Empire, and finally Hitler's territorial ambitions. In light of Germany's history, the Serbian rhetoric of a "Greater Serbia" struck too close to home, providing an added – though not the main – incentive to intervene in order to spoil the Serbian plans.

Some critics have argued that the German government's historically anti-Serbian attitudes played a large role in its uncharacteristically aggressive stance in the Kosovo situation. Matthias Küntzel, a German author and political scientist, wrote that even in the minds of the most enlightened German observers "it was predetermined where the enemy was to be located once again."[16] He claimed that Germany had long been the protector of the Kosovar Liberation Army (KLA), and that it had wanted to bring about the separation of Kosovo from the former Yugoslavia ever since the end of the Cold War. Not only that, but the memory of the Serb contribution to Germany's loss of two World Wars and the fact that Yugoslavia could be considered a "symbol of German defeats"[17] provided added fuel to anti-Serbian sentiments, according to Küntzel.

Although Küntzel's arguments are considered extreme and largely influenced by his own far leftist ideology, there are others who point out the historical animosity between Germans and Serbs.[18] After all, the Greater-Serbian propaganda preceding World War I had already back then led to a very strained relationship between the two nations, exacerbated by Germany's alliance with Austria, whose heir Archduke Franz Ferdinand was shot by a young Serbian patriot. In 1941, the need to help Germany's ally Italy subdue the Serbs pushed back Hitler's invasion of Russia from May to mid-June, with potentially devastating consequences.[19] And even though no one would openly consider that a tragedy in Germany today or even blame the Serbs, the situation in 1999 comes as yet another clash in a long line of hostilities between Germans and Serbs. Finally, Germany's unilateral recognition of Croatia and Slovenia – which some say fueled the flames of the conflict in the Balkans – illustrates Germany's willingness to support anyone but the Serbs, leading to "Serb propaganda that Germany wanted a 4th Reich."[20]

Whatever Germany's motivation, in the public discussion the Serbs were indeed predominantly portrayed as the perpetrators of the conflict from the beginning.[21] In the Media, but also in political speeches and debates, the Serbian police forces and Milošević were compared to the Nazis and Hitler. Considering the enormity of German historical memory, drawing such a parallel inevitably triggered the feeling that "something must be done." Despite a certain cheapening of the analogy by overly frequent (ab)use during the years following the Kosovo conflict, the legacy of World War II was still strong enough to make most Germans pay attention to them.

Finally, German historical memory about the Balkans invariably affected the way politicians felt they should approach the issue. In light of memories of German military aggression in the region, acting within the context of NATO in the case of Kosovo made the use of force more acceptable to audiences at home and abroad. By deliberately constraining German foreign policy through embedding it in multilateral institutions the government was able to act more freely.

German National Interests in Kosovo

Even though I assert that historical memory as part of national identity plays a large role in German foreign policy, it would be wrong to ignore other factors, such as German national interests. Both contribute to the ultimate decision. Without any national interest at stake in the situation, a German participation in the NATO intervention would have been unlikely. Conversely, if historical memory had not allowed such an action, then it would have been very difficult to justify it to audiences at home and abroad. Not only that, but the politicians themselves might have felt compelled to deny participation, as occurred in the early 1990s, when Germany was called on for the first time to help keep the peace in the Balkans.

The definition of German national interests in Kosovo largely remain speculative in nature, as German politicians have not been very forthcoming in giving interest-based explanations in their foreign policy debates. While other countries' leaders have no qualms about citing national interests, national security, and even destiny as reasons for certain actions, Germans have felt the need to use much more idealist rhetoric, such as a concern for human rights, international justice, and even morality.

Nonetheless, it is reasonable to assume that Germany had an interest in ensuring NATO's continued political and military significance. After all, NATO was the only real guarantee of security postwar Germany had ever known. The German Bundeswehr is not only small in numbers, but also not equipped to deal with large-scale security threats on its own. Even though the last (structural) constraints on a military build-up disappeared in 1994 with the official withdrawal of the occupying Allied forces from Berlin, Germany has not made any significant attempts since then to pursue a more independent security policy and to increase its troop size and strength. On the contrary, the Bundeswehr has been consistently decreased in size, and the length of conscription duties for German men – making up the majority of German troops – has been cut from formerly 18 months to only 9 months, which according to many high-ranking officers in the Bundeswehr is not even enough time to train them properly. Currently, two out of three young men in Germany refuse to serve in the military and opt for alternative civil services instead.

Not only that, but the reunified Germany continues to forego autonomy in return for the collective security and burden-sharing NATO provides. Even after reunification, German forces remain highly integrated in NATO's military structures. More so than any other member state's: Germany is the only country whose military is completely assigned to NATO. In addition, as soon as the Two-plus-Four Treaty allowed it, the German government assigned the forces of former East Germany to NATO as well, even though it was not required to do so.[22]

From a utilitarian perspective, this refusal to build up Germany's military and to make it more autonomous makes sense: why increase military spending – probably at the expense of spending in other areas, such as welfare and health insurance – when Germany can "keep its costs of defense low by externalizing some of them on its NATO partners?"[23] At the same time, it creates an undeniable incentive for Germany to keep NATO functional.

Following the end of the Cold War, some questioned the utility of the continued existence of the organization, which, after all, was created to "keep America in, Russia out, and Germany down." NATO quickly found itself in the middle of a crisis of identity.[24] The conflict in Kosovo could be considered a trial for NATO to find a new raison d'état by transforming itself into a regional security and peacekeeping force. As a result, the organization's performance contributes greatly to the perceived need for its continued existence. In their public speeches, German politicians lent weight to this argument by frequently pointing out the need to keep NATO *handlungsfähig* (able to act) and to not jeopardize its credibility as a security alliance.

Perhaps Germany's decision to participate in the airstrikes against Kosovo was the result of a return to an active *Ostpolitik*. Germany had traditionally had strategic interests in the East, mainly as a result of its position as the land of the middle. From such a geopolitical point of view, Germany should be interested in restoring regional stability in the Balkan region. Hans-Dietrich Genscher, former Secretary of State under Helmut Kohl, once said that "because of its geography, Germany will be affected earlier by instability in the East."[25] Hence Germans simply cannot afford to ignore conflicts in Europe's backyard that could potentially spill over. In addition, Germany may wish to restore peace and stability to the Balkans in order to pave the way for a future expansion of NATO – and the EU – eastward. If that were to happen, Germany would simultaneously increase security at the eastern border of Europe and its own. Either that, or Germany is after all seeking to reestablish a central hegemonic position, using the EU and NATO only as an alibi.[26] The push for a military participation in Kosovo could then be seen as part of a "salami tactics" that would slowly get domestic and foreign audiences used to a German return to militarism.

A final German national interest that would be served by a military intervention is that it would prevent a large wave of refugees from entering the country. During the early and mid-1990s, Germany had taken in more refugees from the Balkan region than all other European countries combined. The costs associated with such charity and the fear that a refusal to do so would be interpreted as a resurgence of xenophobia and German nationalism, might provide enough of an incentive to remove the source of the problem (the conflict) as opposed to dealing with its effects (the refugees).

The Political Debates:
Lessons of History and Current Responsibilities

This section traces the political debates accompanying Germany's participation in the airstrikes in the Bundestag, the lower chamber of parliament. It illustrates how the use of force as a means for reaching foreign policy goals has become more acceptable as the result of a political discourse that begins to challenge the basic, anti-militarist narrative of German postwar foreign policy. This "new" rhetoric reinterprets military intervention as a possibility under certain circumstances. Simultaneously, the debates reflect and contribute to the changing nature of historical memory in Germany, due in part to a generational change and in part to an increasing disparity between the traditional interpretation of historical memory and the pressures of the post-Cold War international system.

German foreign policy discourse in the case of Kosovo is heavily characterized by a reliance on particular themes, such as human rights, and a perceived "special" responsibility derived from Germany's history. This responsibility centers on three specific reference points: a responsibility toward democratic values, toward international law, and toward Germany's allies. The speakers are constructing a narrative that justifies the use of force for causes which Germany considers its responsibility. This responsibility is derived from two main sources: the democratic ideals postwar Germany is committed to (as expressed in the Basic Law and in the United Nations Charter) and the lessons of history, derived from Germany's World War II experience. Figure 2.1 shows a rhetorical map – based on frequency counts and a qualitative analysis of the text – of the most important themes in the German Kosovo debates.

Figure 2.1, below, is based on the analysis of eight individual debates,[27] occurring over a time span of seven months. The first, and most important, debate examined here took place on October 16th, 1998. On this occasion, the Bundestag was called in for an unscheduled session in order to discuss the possible military intervention and to decide whether German forces should participate in a potential NATO airstrike against the Serbs. Although the outgoing CDU-FDP government had already made this commitment, it was now up to the newly elected and inaugurated SPD-Greens government to either reaffirm this commitment, or to change the course of German foreign policy in this matter. The second and third debates took place shortly thereafter, on November 13th and November 19th, 1998, and merely served to reinforce the decision made in the previous month.

Figure 2.1: Rhetorical Map of the Kosovo Debates

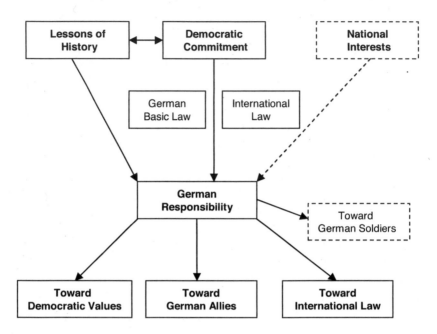

The fourth debate occurred on February 25th, 1999, a little over two weeks after the first round of negotiations at Rambouillet. In the meantime, German soldiers had participated in the United Nations–approved air patrols over former Yugoslavia, monitoring the progress of Milošević' compliance with Resolutions 1160 and 1199 of the Security Council. The February 25th debate was especially interesting, because for the first time since Germany committed to a potential intervention, it looked as though it would indeed come to pass. During the previous debates, much of the rhetoric had focused on the airstrikes as mainly a military threat rather than a reality.

The remaining four debates occurred after the NATO airstrikes had commenced, on March 25th, March 26th, April 15th, and May 7th, 1999. By late March, it had become clear that the negotiations of Rambouillet and Paris have officially failed; Milošević had refused to sign the treaty, and NATO began bombing Serbian targets on March 24th. Originally, the agenda of March 25th had not included a discussion of these events, but as soon as the Bundestag convened, the far-left PDS introduced the motion to expand the agenda in order to allow members of the

Bundestag to respond to the "first German war in 54 years," as Gregor Gysi of the PDS called it. The motion was granted and each party was given the opportunity to give a brief statement about the bombings.

Next to the first debate, the April 15th debate represented the most extensive discussion of the military intervention that took place in the Bundestag. On that occasion, the German government issued a status report in the Bundestag, which was followed by a debate about the progress of the operation. It had now become clear that the humanitarian catastrophe that the airstrikes were supposed to prevent had happened, not despite the intervention, but because of it. According to United Nations reports, 11,000 Kosovar-Albanians were killed by Serbian military and police forces, 863,000 people were driven out of the country, and another 600,000 people were displaced within Kosovo between March 25th 1999 and June 6th 1999. The NATO airstrikes produced another 2,000 military and civilian casualties.

On May 7th, 1999, the Bundestag deliberated a proposal to approve an additional 1,000 Bundeswehr soldiers to be deployed as part of a humanitarian mission ("Allied Harbour") that would bring aid to the refugees in Albania and protect human rights organizations in the area. In addition to the approval of the humanitarian mission, the Bundestag was considering the legitimization of further air patrols in Kosovo, as well as the authorization of German soldiers' use of force for self-defense.

The Lessons of History and German Responsibility

According to the political rhetoric, Germany's unique historical experience and the lessons of history that were derived from it provided one of the main sources of responsibility in the case of Kosovo. Klaus Kinkel (FDP) said that "the lessons of our own history" taught us that "those who do not stop evil become guilty of evil themselves." Simply standing by and watching the horrible events in Kosovo would make the onlookers as guilty as the perpetrators. Volker Rühe (CDU) made this point rather dramatically when he claimed that "watching these terrible scenes on TV in Western Europe without acting would be tantamount to cutting up our own face with a rusty razor blade and to disfiguring it ... It is a matter of our credibility." Joschka Fischer (Greens) added that "if we have learned the lessons of our history and of the bloody first half of the 20th century, then there must not be any more war mongering in Europe." Wolfgang Gerhardt (FDP) pointed out that the Bundestag always acts "in awareness and knowledge of German history in this century," implying that the past continues to influence the present.

What made these lessons of history so important to many Bundestag members was the fact that many of them, and even more of their voters, were old enough to personally remember the horrors of war. In the past, Germany's special responsibility to avoid war had often been framed in those terms. How could someone who had personally lived through a terrible war sit back and watch it happen anywhere else? In addition, there were many Germans who became refugees themselves after German capitulation in 1945, when they were forced to leave their homes across Eastern Europe in retribution for Germany's war crimes. The memory of their experiences was being kept alive in German schools and in the Media, making it reasonable to assume that it would resurface in the political debates in a case such as this.

In the past, Germany's history had often been cited in the Bundestag as a reason to not intervene militarily abroad, especially in regions where Wehrmacht soldiers had played an active role during WW II. In this case, the opposite was true. Gerhard Schröder (SPD) argued that "the fact that Germany under a criminal regime became guilty in the Balkans, does not allow the democratic Germany of today to let crimes happen there in that part of Europe – on the contrary!" Klaus Kinkel (FDP) said that Germany had a responsibility to free the Kosovar-Albanians from Serbian oppression, because Germans can not have forgotten that they themselves "were not able to free themselves from a tyrant, but rather had to be freed forcefully by others." Volker Rühe (CDU) admitted that there "are examples in history that show that it can be immoral to use soldiers; in other situations, however, one has to say that it is deeply immoral to not use soldiers, when it is the only chance to stop war and massacre." He implied that an immoral activity in one setting (the Wehrmacht in the Balkans in 1943) can be moral in another setting (the Bundeswehr in the Balkans in 1999).

With regard to the duty to promote peace and stability in the Balkans, German history was cited by Dr. Wolfgang Schäuble (CDU), when he pointed out that Germany's "history of this century shows that the step to a disruption of peace in international relations is a small one, and [therefore] we have to be willing to secure the peace."

For the first time, Germany had a chance to be on the right side of an international conflict and a chance to right a wrong. Rudolf Scharping (SPD) reminded the Bundestag that it was in a unique position to "give hope to those who have escaped terror and brutality," creating not merely an opportunity but a "responsibility ... because of our own history." Christian Schmidt (CDU) added that this "has to do with our collective memories, with the fact that there are many people who know firsthand what it is like when one has to leave one's home with nothing but a suitcase and bare necessities."

A second important source of German responsibility that was highlighted in many of the speeches was Germany's democratic commitment, which can be defined as a commitment to all the democratic values expressed in the German *Grundgesetz* (Basic Law) and to the United Nations Charter as the locus of international law. The latter is particularly important as the source for universal human rights, which in turn cause the German responsibility to act on behalf of those rights. "International law does not enforce itself," said Wolfgang Gerhardt (FDP). Instead, it is the responsibility of states to not look away when human rights are violated, and to make sure that justice prevails. Klaus Kinkel (FDP) spoke of the necessity to accept "responsibility for peace and human rights." Günter Verheugen (SPD) pointed out that international law had arrived at a point at which the systematic violation of human rights has become a basis for action. It was international law that allowed Germany to participate in this mission and Germany's historical experiences that compelled it.

In addition to international law, Bundestag members cited Germany's own Basic Law as a basis for action. Klaus Kinkel (FDP) reminded the Bundestag that "in the Basic Law, the German people express their commitment to the inviolable and inalienable human rights as the basis for every society." If human rights are violated anywhere in the world, it is the duty of those who believe in the Basic Law to act. He added that especially the German people know the importance of protecting human rights. In fact, one need look no further than the very first sentence of the Basic Law to realize the truth of this: "Die Würde des Menschen is unantastbar" (The dignity of human beings must not be violated).

Despite this passionate plea, it should be kept in mind that although the Basic Law had emphasized the importance of human rights for almost fifty years by the time the problems in Kosovo arose, the Bundestag had not interpreted this as a duty to intervene militarily to stop human rights violations up until that point. Even though the concern for the rights of the Kosovar-Albanians appeared genuine enough, it would be naïve to assume that it was the only reason for the Bundestag's decision. Nonetheless, Germany's commitment to democratic ideals goes hand in hand with the lessons of history, as the former is in a sense a result of the latter.

German Responsibility in Kosovo

One of the most interesting themes of the debates was that of responsibility, which the speakers cite as their primary motivation for approving the military intervention. The notion of responsibility as a driving force in foreign policy had long permeated political rhetoric in Germany. Almost from its inception, the Federal Republic's self-understanding was characterized by a perceived need to behave as and be considered a responsible nation that has learned the lessons of history. One of the first and most important goals during the immediate postwar period was to regain the trust of the international community and to prove that Germany could be a reliable, democratic partner. Chancellor Konrad Adenauer and his successors therefore developed a new, history-friendly approach that relied on diplomacy and the practice of a responsible and moral foreign policy.

Former Secretary of State Hans-Dietrich Genscher coined the term *Verantwortungspolitik* (politics of responsibility) which soon became a catchword of German foreign policy rhetoric.[28] In the same vein, Willy Brandt and Helmut Schmidt frequently drew a connection between the German past and the necessity of an active *Friedenspolitik* (politics of peace) that was guided by a sense of responsibility. The almost obsessively idealist rhetoric of almost all postwar politicians once led Johannes Gross, a German satirist, to remark that "the word 'Realpolitik' has been lost in the German language and will no longer be needed; it lives on in other languages as a foreign expression. In place of it, we urgently need the word 'Moralpolitik' in order to label that which we, out of responsibility, refrain from doing."[29] German philosopher Jürgen Habermas also wrote extensively about the concept of responsibility in German politics, arguing that in light of their history, Germans had a responsibility to remember the war and the Holocaust, and to draw the correct consequences from both for their future actions[30].

In the Kosovo debates, Joschka Fischer (Greens) drew on this long tradition when he spoke of a "special responsibility for the reunited Germany." Michael Glos (CDU) praised the decision to participate in the mission as a sign that the "government has taken on responsibility, has decided resolutely, and has fulfilled its duty." His fellow party member Volker Rühe (CDU) reminded the Bundestag that because of Germany's history and its long practice of a responsible and moral foreign policy, "[e]veryone must know that here lies a special responsibility." He was echoed by Gerhard Schröder (SPD) who said that "[W]e cannot avoid our responsibility." For the new chancellor

Schröder to make such a statement is particularly meaningful, because it shows that the newly elected government will honor the outgoing government's previously made commitment.

In the specific case of Kosovo, there was an even more immediate and direct responsibility that compelled Germany to intervene. Christian Schmidt (CDU) argued that because Germany had been involved in the peace process in the Balkans for several years, it would have to see it through to the end or risk losing all credibility in the eyes of the international community. "As a member of the Balkan Contact Group," he said, "we have a special responsibility." According to Dr. Wolfgang Schäuble (CDU), Germans "know [their] responsibility there." And Otto Schily the new Secretary of the Interior (SPD) said that "the crisis in Kosovo – we know this, ladies and gentlemen – has placed a very grave responsibility on Germany."

Germany's Responsibility to Uphold Democratic Values

I argued above that the interpretation of what such a responsibility entails varies over time. Nonetheless there is a certain constant in most German foreign policy debates in that they all tend to follow the same rhetorical map (cf. figure 2.1). One of the three main reference points of German responsibility is democratic values. In the Kosovo debates, the values most frequently addressed were peace in the Balkans and the human rights of the Kosovar-Albanians. The speeches were permeated by many graphic accounts of the violations these people had had to suffer at the hands of the Serbian perpetrators.

On the basis of vivid reports of the suffering in the many refugee camps, most speakers considered it imperative to act, and to do so before it was too late. Wolfgang Gerhardt (FDP) appealed to the morality – and the emotions – of his colleagues when he stated that the members of the Bundestag were deciding no less than the "fate of the people in Kosovo," a fate that at this point in time seemed to consist of "suffering, need, hunger, flight, and a desolate situation." Michael Glos (CDU/CSU) was no less dramatic in his appeal that the Bundestag was charged with the "prevention of a humanitarian catastrophe," with the "saving of human lives," and with the "ending of human suffering." Other speakers focused on the "brutality of the Serbian military,"[31] the occurrence of "murder, expulsion, and unspeakable suffering,"[32] and the "aggressive nationalism" of the Serbs against the Albanian minority.[33] All these accounts painted a very dramatic and gruesome picture of the Kosovar-Albanians' situation.

It is interesting to note how much the debates focused on the human dimension of the situation, as opposed to political or security concerns. Although the situation in Kosovo certainly posed a certain threat to Germany and the rest of Europe due to its potential to destabilize the entire region and to cause a wave of refugees that were likely to seek entrance into the European Union, these concerns were not nearly as prominent in the German debates as the concern for human lives and human rights.

The protection of human rights was referenced as the main motivation for Germany's participation in the military intervention. Indeed, it was considered to be the only acceptable motivation for participation by many members of the Bundestag. Ulrich Irmer (FDP) illustrated this when he said that his party had "always emphasized that the use of the military is only legitimate if it serves the protection of human rights". Christian Schwarz-Schilling (CDU/CSU) added that "human rights enjoy primacy over other factors" in this decision. One of his colleagues went even further when he argued that this military intervention served "the most important of all purposes, namely the protection of human rights and the safeguarding of human dignity," wherein "lies the true legitimization of ... the German participation."[34] At the same time, the speakers made it very clear that the use of any type of force for the attainment of political goals remained completely unacceptable.

As time went on and it became clear that the implementation of a political solution had not been successful, NATO implemented the plan to use military means to protect the people in Kosovo. The continued fighting and especially "the massacre of Račak forced the international community to reach peace first against and then hopefully with the participants."[35] Germany could not escape this conflict by looking away; instead, the "drama – the murder, the destruction, and the refugees – ultimately force one to take notice and to intervene." Eberhardt Brecht (SPD) reaffirmed Germany's responsibility when he said that "we must not stand by and watch such a brutal conflict right in front of our door." Helmut Lippelt (Bündnis 90/Die Grünen) added that it was imperative to "stop the murder, which has already begun, before it reaches its zenith."

Approving the airstrikes was the right course of action, because Germany "can not and must not continue to watch as the majority of citizens in Kosovo are forced out and murdered."[36] The Serbian army was brutally slaughtering innocent civilians, more than 400,000 people had fled their homes, villages were burning.[37] Germany simply could not ignore these facts, the majority of Bundestag members argued. "It is our duty to stop [this] and to ensure that the people in Kosovo receive a chance at a peaceful life."[38] If Germany takes seriously its "responsibility for peace, for freedom, and for human rights, then there is no alternative" to the airstrikes.[39] Germany's goal in Kosovo was "not aggressive, not hostile. We want international guarantees for human rights there."[40]

The frequent reference to Germany's history as a source for this responsibility toward human rights was noticeable. "It is a responsibility on the basis of our experiences in the first half of this century," Rudolf Scharping (SPD) argued. He added that one could not allow the "grimace of the wars of the first half of the century" to dominate the future. The region of the Balkans "has made very many experiences with terror, oppression, and violence," and it needs help to move into the future. Dr. Wolfgang Gerhardt (FDP) agreed that "after all the experiences in this century, there can be no alternative for a free democracy than to meet an aggressor, even with soldiers."

Much of the rhetoric seemed designed to remind the audience – Bundestag members, but also the German public – that the airstrikes that seemed cruel and terrible had a justified cause. It would have been "fatal, if Milošević' cynical plan had worked out."[41] "Expulsion, ethnic cleansing, and genocide must not be tolerated, especially not within Europe."[42] Peter Struck (SPD) called Milošević an "insane, power-hungry dictator" with the "racist goal of an 'ethnically clean' Serbia." Milošević' was a "campaign of murder and expulsion." Right from the start he had been planning a "crusade of ethnic cleansing ... which has so far cost thousands of lives in Kosovo."[43] The occurrence of "genocide" created a "duty to intervene." Especially "in the face of universal human rights the classical nonintervention policy must not become a blank check for dictators to murder and expel their own population."[44] Human rights had to be protected, even if doing so meant going against international law. Along with the reaffirmation of the just cause, many of the speakers pointed out repeatedly how "necessary" this intervention was, how there was "no alternative," and how the Bundestag "had to" act. The "use of military force is necessary and politically and morally justifiable."[45]

Because this was such a milestone in German history – one of the Bundestag members compared it to Caesar crossing the Rubicon – the Bundestag members were trying to avoid any negative parallels to WW II, but rather emphasized how it was exactly those experiences more than five decades prior and the lessons learned from them that now formed the basis for this intervention.

Another dimension of Germany's responsibility toward democratic values centered on the protection and restoration of peace in the Balkan region. It fell to Germany as a member of the Western community of states to restore the peace that Milošević and the Serbs had broken. "It is necessary to implement peaceful rules and to enable a peaceful life" for the Kosovar-Albanians, Joschka Fischer (Greens) said. "Without peace in the Balkans, no part of Europe will find rest," according to Ulrich Irmer (FDP). Dr. Wolfgang Schäuble (FDP) argued that Germany had "to be willing to protect fundamental human rights and peace; through integration, through regionalization, and if necessary through the use of military force." Interestingly, while the German Bundestag had always considered peace one of its primary foreign policy goals, in the past, this had been interpreted as a need to preserve the peace by refusing to use any military force. By 1999, this had apparently been reinterpreted to allow for an active enforcement and restoration of peace.

Germany's Responsibility toward Its Allies

A second reference point for German responsibility was that toward its allies. Part of Adenauer's plan to regain the trust of the international community after the foundation of the Federal Republic had been to establish an image of Germany as a reliable and credible partner. Naturally, Germany's neighbors were very skeptical and apprehensive during the time following the end of World War II. One can understand why, considering the country's history of making and breaking alliances, Hitler's politics of appeasement preceding the war, and the brutality with which the war was fought. As a result, reliability, predictability, and transparency above all else became the guiding principles of German foreign policy.

After decades of emphasizing these values in German foreign policy rhetoric, it is not surprising that in the Kosovo debates much emphasis was placed on the need to support Germany's NATO partners. The members of the Bundestag portrayed the situation in a way that suggested that NATO had already made the decision to intervene militarily in Kosovo, and that for Germany to not support this decision would be fatal for NATO and would constitute a grave violation of Germany's responsibility to stand by its allies. NATO had to be "able to rely on the solidarity of the unified Germany."[46]

An element of urgency was added by the fact that Germany's "NATO partners, whose governments are already standing firmly behind the planned airstrikes, are waiting for a clear decision by the German Bundestag," as Volker Rühe (FDP) pointed out. The decision to intervene in Kosovo, he added, was not only important for the protection of human rights and international law, but also as "an expression of

Germany's solidarity in the alliance." Some of the speakers even claimed indecision or inactivity by the Bundestag might seriously endanger the credibility, and even the survival, of NATO as an organization. Gerhard Schröder (SPD), for instance, said that only after "it became clear that Germany's capacity to act was not limited and that NATO was therefore able to back up its military threat, Milošević showed signs of giving in." He implied that NATO without Germany's support would be unable to act. Dr. Eberhardt Brecht (SPD) emphasized that "the implementation of the ... treaty [of Rambouillet] must not fail due to the lack of willingness on the part of NATO-member Germany." To hesitate in this matter, or worse, to not reach an agreement at all, would be tantamount to Germany's "isolation in the alliance," according to Rudolf Scharping (SPD), the new Secretary of Defense.

Much of the responsibility toward Germany's allies, i.e. NATO, was derived from German history. Not only was being a reliable partner necessary in order to regain and keep the trust of the international community, but it was also an expression of gratitude to those who had helped Germany in its hour of need. Its allies had to be able to rely on Germany, "just as we were able to rely on NATO in other respects for decades," said Klaus Kinkel (FDP). The United States in particular "has always stood faithfully by us and by Europe," which is why "hopefully the Bundestag will send a signal of reliability today," according to Michael Glos (CDU). "Until Milošević complies [with the ultimatum], and until the return of the refugees is guaranteed, he needs to know that NATO is capable to act at any moment, and that Germany will make its contribution."

Germany's Responsibility toward International Law

In addition to a responsibility toward democratic values and toward its allies, Germany also had a self-declared responsibility toward international law. While the above-mentioned human rights could certainly be considered an integral part of international law as explicated in the United Nations Charter, this specific responsibility went beyond that. It included the right of a people to self-determination, to freedom from oppression, the prevention and punishment of the illegitimate use of force, and the commitment to the promotion of peace, stability, and democracy abroad.

In the past, Germany had always verbally expressed its commitment to these international law ideals and had abided by them itself, but had never ventured beyond offering political or financial support for their defense. The most "extreme" action the Bundestag took in this regard up until Kosovo was the unilateral recognition of Croatia's and Slovenia's independence in 1991, to the astonishment of much of the international community. Whether this was the expression of a genuine belief in the right to self-determination or whether the decision was influenced by ulterior motives is not clear.

In the Kosovo debates, several speakers expressed their conviction that the illegitimate use of force by Milošević – a direct violation of international law – had to be stopped. "There must be no blank check for the use of tanks and artillery against one's own people. Violence must not pay off in Europe," said Volker Rühe (FDP). Gerhard Schröder (SPD) demanded from the Serbian leadership to "enter the road to democratic and lawful reforms" and to "meet the European norms and standards." Joschka Fischer (Greens) argued that one had to put a stop to Belgrade's legally and "ethically not justifiable, aggressive nationalist politics."

What makes the case of Kosovo so interesting is that even though the Bundestag members cited the protection of international law and universal human rights as the basis for this intervention, the mission was actually in violation of international law, as there was no United Nations resolution that authorized the NATO airstrikes. It was very surprising that Germany showed such willingness to go against the United Nations, considering its usual reticence.

The speakers were very aware of this contradiction. Most of them addressed the lack of a United Nations mandate at least briefly. The overriding consensus in the matter was that although the lack of a mandate was regrettable, it did not constitute an insurmountable obstacle to the intervention. Instead, the violation of international law – which many speakers actually recognized as such – was portrayed as a necessity resulting from an earlier and much graver violation on the part of Milošević and the Serbian army. In other words, when compared to the violation of human rights, the NATO-led intervention was a less grave offense and directly caused by the Serbian offense. In some instances, the speakers even referred to the intervention as a duty, or as a service to the United Nations, saving the organization from the stalemate it found itself in.

NATO had taken it upon itself to defend human rights, even in the face of "the Security Council's inability to utilize its monopoly of violence," according to Wolfgang Gerhardt (FDP). In light of this context, the intervention " is not an arbitrary act by NATO, if it [NATO] does not want humans to suffer, to freeze, to have to flee, or to die from hunger, simply because a few heads of state are not capable of …utilizing their monopoly of violence."[47] Other speakers agreed with this assessment that human rights should take precedence over state sovereignty and ironically even international law itself, if there is a conflict of interest. Rudolf Scharping (SPD), for instance, argued that even though the legal basis for this action was questionable, inaction in the face of such grave human rights violations would have been worse. He went as far as asking whether the United Nations as a Cold War institution was even capable of enforcing universal human rights, or whether one should not consider a reform of international law that would reflect the importance of universal human rights and the responsibility derived therefrom.

Many did not even consider the NATO-intervention a breach of international law *per se*, but rather an attempt to "help" the United Nations. Günter Verheugen (SPD) called it an "emergency situation, in which the actual holder of the monopoly of violence is unable to act." Gernot Erler (SPD) added that despite concerns about the legality of the mission, he believed that it was necessary to promote a world order in which the power of the law triumphs over the law of the most powerful. Most of the speakers claimed that though they were not acting within the legal boundaries of the United Nations Charter, they were acting in its "spirit."

Nevertheless, a sense of unease remained, which was perhaps best illustrated by the fact that most speakers expressed their hope that the threat of airstrikes against the Serbs would be sufficient to make Milošević give in. Much credence was given to the notion of *Drohpotential* (deterrence potential) and to the belief that if NATO appeared decisive and determined enough, Milošević would ultimately give in, making a military intervention unnecessary. As Wolfang Gerhardt (FDP) put it, "We are assuming and hoping that it [the military intervention] will not be necessary." Joschka Fischer (Bündnis 90/Die Grünen) added, "we are all hoping – and thank God with legitimate cause – that it will never have to happen and will never happen." Ironic as it may seem, the Bundestag expressed the belief that by authorizing the NATO airstrikes it was paving the way for a peaceful solution of the conflict.

Some Differences in the Rhetoric

An analysis of the political rhetoric across party lines reveals a perhaps surprising amount of consensus, with the notable exception of the *Partei Deutscher Sozialisten* (PDS). Almost all other speakers agreed on the basic themes of the debates: that Germany had a responsibility to enforce human rights, that despite legal difficulties the NATO mission was justifiable, and that the use of military force for humanitarian purposes was acceptable, but not for political or other goals.

In contrast, the PDS speakers pointed out the illegality of the mission. Gregor Gysi (PDS), for instance, lamented that most of his colleagues "pretend that [the use of force] is an entirely legitimate tool, even though the UN Charter prohibits even the threat of use of force." He added that only the Security Council was able to authorize the use of force, as it holds the monopoly of violence. For the Bundestag to claim that a military intervention in Kosovo would be in the spirit of the United Nations did not mask the fact that it was breaking international law. Uwe-Jens Heuer (PDS) stated that he would vote against the intervention mainly due to legal reasons. He pointed out that "there is no mandate ... therefore there is no legal basis for the mission."

Along the same lines, the PDS members insisted that this intervention was setting a precedent in international law that might be abused in the future. Gregor Gysi claimed that "NATO has set a precedent, and the Bundestag is today creating a precedent" as well. Even though the rest of the Bundestag might claim that this was not the case, Gysi pointed out that "whether something is a precedent or not is not decided by the one setting it, but by the other countries in the world." By going against the United Nations, Germany was opening the door for future abuses of military interventions.

Gysi even accused the Bundestag of being fully aware of this matter. He considered the decision to participate in the airstrikes part of a grand strategy that was contributing to a "worldwide militarization of international relations and foreign policy." The Bundestag was utilizing so-called "salami tactics" to slowly remove all barriers to the use of the German military abroad, and it is using human rights as a vehicle to do so (ibid.).

Foreign Policy Rhetoric: "Young" vs. "Old"
In the introduction, I argued that a certain generational effect could be expected to take place with regard to historical memory in Germany. When examining the rhetoric of younger vs. older Bundestag members, some interesting patterns emerge. Unfortunately, these findings are constrained by two facts: (1) although there are quite a few members of the Bundestag who are fairly young (i.e. who were born during the late 1950s or 1960s), they do not generally have the opportunity to speak in front of the parliament, because the more senior members of each party are given preference, and (2) the majority of "younger" speakers are members of the Greens, which is likely to bias any analysis because of the very liberal and pacifist attitudes generally shared by those who join

a party such as the Greens in the first place. Table 2.1 shows the age divisions of the 13th Bundestag.

Table 2.1: Age Divisions of the 13th German Bundestag (1994-1998)

Birth Year	Men						Women						BT total
	CDU	SPD	GR	FDP	PDS	total	CDU	SPD	GR	FDP	PDS	total	
1911-1915	-	-	-	-	1	1	-	-	-	-	-	-	1
1916-1920	1	-	-	-	-	1	-	-	-	-	-	-	1
1921-1925	-	-	-	-	2	2	-	-	-	-	-	-	2
1926-1930	7	4	-	4	1	16	1	1	-	-	-	-	18
1931-1935	24	11	1	4	3	43	4	2	-	2	-	8	51
1936-1940	58	44	1	7	-	110	8	18	-	1	1	28	138
1941-1945	66	60	2	12	1	141	10	22	5	2	1	40	181
1946-1950	33	27	8	9	4	81	11	21	5	1	3	41	122
1951-1955	33	15	3	2	4	57	4	12	8	1	3	28	85
1956-1960	18	3	3	1	-	25	1	7	6	-	4	18	43
1961-1965	13	2	1	-	-	16	1	2	3	1	1	8	24
1966-1970	-	1	-	-	1	2	1	-	2	-	-	3	5
1971-1975	-	-	1	-	-	-	-	-	-	-	-	-	1
Total	253	167	20	39	17	496	41	85	29	8	13	176	672

Source: German Bundestag, 2006
BT = Bundestag
CDU = Christian Democratic Union
FDP = Free Democratic Party
GR = GreensSPD = Social Democratic Party
PDS = Part of Democratic Socialism

Despite the limitations of the data, it is interesting that the younger Bundestag members did not speak of German national interests any more frequently – less, in fact – than did the rest. It might have been expected that they would have fewer inhibitions due to the fact that they had all been born well after the end of World War II, and therefore might feel that the guilt shared by the older generations does not apply to them. Instead, they emphasized the importance of "responsibility" more often frequently. If that were indeed indicative of this entire age group, then one of two conclusions applies: (1) either the generational effect simply has not yet occurred, or (2) Germany's transformation to a civilian power is truly genuine and even though military intervention has become possible under certain circumstances, it could not be justified for the pursuit of national interests.

German Foreign Policy Action:
Troops in Kosovo – Déjà vu?

The NATO-led military intervention "Allied Force" began on March 24th, 1999. It lasted 78 days and had two goals: (1) to force the Milošević regime to sign the agreement of Rambouillet, which outlined a 3-year interim solution to the conflict, and (2) to prevent a humanitarian catastrophe. Germany contributed 14 Tornadoes of the Bundeswehr, which constituted the first time since the end of World War II that Germany had become militarily active in an offensive combat mission.

One of the most striking characteristics of the debates was the heavy reliance on idealist language and the concept of a responsible foreign policy in the service of human rights. One might question whether the talk matched the actions. In other words, was the idealist rhetoric used merely as camouflage for more realist interests?

At a first glance, it might appear that the actions indeed did not completely match the talk. Even though the rhetoric was highly idealistic, the way the military intervention was carried out was rather realist in nature. NATO did not send ground troops, but rather limited its actions to airstrikes. This was likely the result of the desire to minimize casualties and to achieve the maximum outcome with the minimum input, an approach which matches the basic tenets of Realism. While airstrikes were efficient, they also jeopardized the civilian population. Indeed, according to United Nations reports, the humanitarian catastrophe that NATO members had claimed they wanted to avoid occurred not despite but rather as a result of the airstrikes. The question that inevitably arises is that if the German Bundestag really was concerned with human rights, why did it risk the suffering of innocent civilians by choosing to participate in the airstrikes rather than sending ground troops?

The cynical answer to the question is that the rhetoric of responsibility was "cheap" and that the Bundestag was not really as worried about the protection of human rights as it claimed. While there is no way to prove this argument – or disprove it, for that matter – I do not believe this to be entirely true. While the airstrikes might not have been the ideal approach, they did force Milošević to give in to the demands of NATO and the United Nations in the end. Perhaps members of the Bundestag thought this was their only option to make him comply, which seems a reasonable assumption considering that Milošević had made and broken promises over and over again for several years. Another factor to consider is that German politicians perhaps felt as though it would be easier to "sell" a limited intervention to the German public than to have the first mission after more than 50 years of "abstinence" be an all-out intervention.

The amount of humanitarian aid Germany gave to Kosovo also speaks against the notion that the Bundestag did not care about human rights. This indicates that the talk about human rights was not just empty talk, but that there was a genuine concern for the fate of the refugees. The same is true for Germany's policy toward the refugees. While there was a certain reluctance to open the doors to an unlimited number of refugees, German did take in more refugees than any other European nation. When it became clear in May 1999 that Kosovo's neighbors Albania and Macedonia were overwhelmed by the waves of refugees, it was Germany which started a campaign to push the EU to accept more refugees.

The Changing Nature of German Responsibility: A Precedent for the Future?

The eight debates accompanying the military intervention in Kosovo were driven by the above-explained "responsibility" talk in all its dimensions. As pointed out earlier, this emphasis on responsibility is nothing new in German foreign policy. What is interesting about the case of Kosovo, however, is that while responsibility is still driving German foreign policy rhetoric, the interpretation of that responsibility appears to have changed.

Until only a few years ago, for example, one aspect of a responsible Germany was the reluctance to use the military as a foreign policy tool. In the current Kosovo debate, the concept for the first time entailed the use of military force – not despite Germany's responsibility, but because of it. The Bundestag appears to have re-constructed the meaning of responsibility, from a pacifist approach to foreign policy to a "responsible" use of the German military. Figure 2.2 illustrates the changed nature of German responsibility.

Figure 2.2: The Changing Nature of German Responsibility

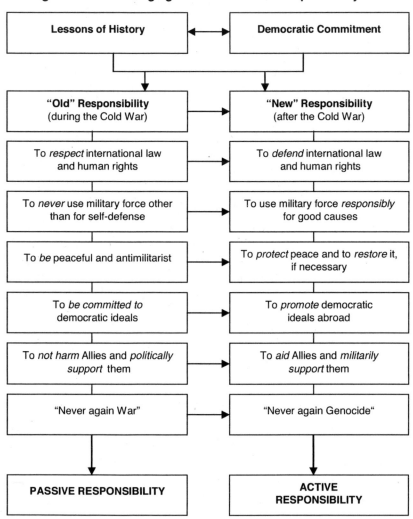

The major difference between the old and the new responsibility is that its interpretation used to be much more passive than it is now. Whereas Germans used to consider it their responsibility to respect international law and human rights, they now consider it their duty to defend international law and human rights, if necessary. The vow to never use military force other than for self-defense has turned into a vow to use military force responsibly, i.e. for a good cause and within the framework of a multilateral alliance or institution. While being peaceful used to be considered the ultimate goal, Germans appear to have realized that in some instances it may become necessary to protect peace and to restore it, rather than merely practice it. Likewise, being committed to democratic ideals has turned into a responsibility to promote these same democratic ideals abroad. A promise to not harm German allies and to politically support them has become a duty to aid German allies and to militarily support them, should the situation call for it. The decade-old slogan "Never again War," still flaunted so proudly during the 1991 Gulf War and during the crisis in Bosnia, has given way to the slogan "Never again Genocide" with all the consequences this brings with it. Passive responsibility has become active responsibility.

What has not changed is the source of responsibility. Before and after, both the commitment to democratic ideals and the lessons of history remain the most influential sources of German responsibility. The exact nature of the lessons learned and the consequences that flow from them as well as from Germany's democratic commitment have been re-interpreted, however.

It appears that certain elements of German foreign policy discourse are – as of yet – unchangeable. While the Bundestag members can re-interpret exactly what responsibility means, it has to do so within certain boundaries. Most importantly, the concept has to be reconciled with Germany's World War II experience, as do the resulting foreign policy actions. If the Bundestag – in its debates – is able to construct a meaning of responsibility that allows the use of military force and is reconcilable with Germany's past, then military intervention can once again be considered as a foreign policy tool. Historical memory is undergoing a definite change in Germany, but such change has to remain incremental in nature.

---

[1] Red = Social Democratic Party of Germany (SPD); Green = BÜNDNIS 90/Die Grünen (Greens)

[2] Rudolf Scharping (1999). *Wir dürfen nicht wegsehen. Der Kosovo-Krieg und Europa.* Berlin; Gregor Schöllgen (1993). *Angst vor der Macht: Die Deutschen und ihre Außenpolitik.* Berlin: Ullstein; Adrian Hyde-Price (1999). "Berlin Republic Takes to Arms," *The World Today* (June); "Alle Serben im Krieg," *Der Spiegel*, No. 13, March 29 1999, p. 196; [2] "Stopping the Catastrophe," *Newsweek*, April 26 1999, p. 29.

[3] *Machtpolitik* can be translated as the realist concept of "power politics," while *Drang nach Osten* refers to Germany's previously exhibited "urge to expand Eastward." Authors who view Germany's participation in Kosovo in a negative light include: Heinz Loquai (2000). *Der Kosovo-Konflikt: Wege in einen vermeidbaren Krieg. Die Zeit von Ende November 1997 bis März 1999.* Baden-Baden; Berthold Meyer and Peter Schlotter (2000). *Die Kosovo-Kriege 1998/99. Die internationalen Interventionen und ihre Folgen.* HSFK-Report 1/2000. Frankfurt/M.; Wolf-Dieter Narr, Roland Roth, and.Klaus Vack (1999). *Wider die kriegerischen Menschenreche: Eine pazifistisch-menschenrechtliche Streitschrift. Beispiel: Kosovo 1999 – NATO-Krieg gegen Jugoslawien.* Komitee für Grundrechte und Freiheiten, Köln; Matthias Küntzel (2000). *Der Weg in den Krieg: Deutschland, die NATO und das Kosovo.* Berlin: Elefantenpress.

[4] Rudolf Scharping (SPD), for instance, said in 1995 that German military participation in the Balkan region was entirely inappropriate "because of the German past." Ironically he was one of the most adamant proponents for the airstrikes in Kosovo, also "because of the German past."

[5] See Carl Lankowski, ed., (1999). Breakdown, Breakup, Breakthrough: *Germany's Difficult Passage to Modernity.* New York: Berghahn Books, p. 56 f.; Also: Anthony Glees (1996). Reinventing Germany: German Political Development since 1945. Dulles, VA: Berg, p. 274. (This reluctance is partly explained by the fact that almost 80 % of Germans at the time were against committing troops to former Yugoslavia, even more than in the case of the 1991 Gulf War.)

[6] 74th Session of the Bundestag, November 30th, 1995: Voigt, p. 6457.

[7] Ibid.: Irmer, 6645 (emphasis added).

[8] Ibid.

[9] 74th Session of the Bundestag: Schulz, 6665.

[10] Ibid.: Verheugen, p. 6666.

[11] Ibid.: Gerhardt, p. 6441.

[12] Ibid.: p. 6440.

[13] Adrian Hyde-Price, p. 21.

[14] Of course this does not apply to the Serbs who considered any interference by the West as a violation of their state sovereignty. In an interview with a German TV station, Bosnian-Serb leader Radovan Karadzic even warned of the "unimaginable consequences" if German soldiers were to be seen in the Balkans.

[15] Cf. Hagen Schulze (1998). *Germany: A New History.* Cambridge, MA: Harvard University Press, pp. 125 ff.

[16] Küntzel (2000). *Der Weg in den Krieg*, p. 10.

[17] Ibid., p. 184.

[18] Cf. Gordon A. Craig (1971). *Europe since 1815.* Harcourt College Publication; Volker Rittberger, ed., (2001). *German Foreign Policy since Unification: Theories and Case Studies.* Manchester, UK: Manchester University Press.

[19] Scott Erb (2003). *German Foreign Policy: Navigating a New Era.* Boulder, CO: Lynne Rienner Publishers, p. 155.

[20] Ibid., p. 159.

[21] See Holm Sundhaussen (2000). "Kosovo: Eine Konfliktgeschichte," in: Konrad Clewing and Jens Reuter, eds.: *Der Kosovo-Konflikt: Ursachen – Akteure – Verlauf.* Bayerische Landeszentrale für politische Bildung: München, p. 65-88; Günter Joetze (2001). *Der letzte Krieg in Europa? Das Kosovo und die deutsche Politik.* München, p. 24f.; Heinz Loquai (2003). "Medien als Weichensteller zum Krieg," Referat während der Sommerakademie auf Burg Schlaining (Austria).

[22] Bulletin des Presse- und Informationsamtes der Bundesregierung, 1/95, p. 3.

[23] Volker Rittberger (2001). German Foreign Policy since Reunification, p. 149.

[24] See Joseph Lepgold (1998). "NATO's Post-Cold War Collective Action Problem," *International Security*, Vol. 23, No. 1 (Summer) 1998, pp. 78-106.

[25] Ibid., p. 138.

[26] Wolfgang Wessels (2001). "Germany's Power and the Weakening of States in a Globalised World. Deconstructing a Paradox," in: Douglas Webber, *New Europe, New Germany*, p. 107.

[27] Transcribed and published on the Internet site of the German Bundestag.

[28] See Mertes, Müller, Winkler (1996). *In Search of Germany* for a detailed analysis of the so-called "jargon of harmony" that makes up German foreign policy rhetoric.

[29] Gross, Johannes (1993). "Notizbuch Johannes Gross. Neueste Folge," *FAZ-Magazin*, 26 February 1993, p. 10.

[30] See Jürgen Habermas 1989 and 1994.

[31] Klaus Kinkel (then Secretary of State).

[32] Gerhard Schröder (SPD).

[33] Joschka Fischer (Bündnis 90/Die Grünen).

[34] Kurt Rossmanith (CDU).

[35] Joschka Fischer, Secretary of State.

[36] Wolfgang Thierse (President of the Bundestag).

[37] Rudolph Scharping (SPD); see similar assessments by Angelika Beer (Bündnis 90/Die Grünen) and Wolfgang Gerhardt (FDP).

[38] Rudolph Scharping (SPD).

[39] Wolfgang Thierse (President of the BT).

[40] Wolfgang Gerhardt (FDP).

[41] Wolfgang Schäuble (CDU/CSU).

[42] ibid.

[43] Gerhard Schröder (Chancellor).

[44] Wolfgang Schäuble (CDU/CSU).

[45] Gerhard Schröder (SPD).

[46] Klaus Kinkel, Secretary of State.

[47] Ibid.

3
A Trajectory of Change?
The Case of Afghanistan

"Men who fear witches
soon find themselves surrounded by them;
men who become jealous of private property,
soon encounter eager thieves."
— Kai Erikson, *Wayward Puritans*[1]

Germany's participation in the Kosovo intervention was interpreted as a major step on the road to normalcy.[2] According to some, the KFOR mission served to "solidify the new consensus"[3] on German foreign policy at the turn of the millennium, a consensus based on the abandonment of many of the traditional doubts about the use of military force as a foreign policy tool. As such, Kosovo could be seen as a defining moment in the politics of Germany, illustrating a new attitude among the political elite that had turned them from "a bunch of bumbling amateurs to a bunch of determined hawks."[4] If that were true, then Germany should in the future be expected to continue this transformation into a "normal" power that is not afraid to engage in military operations, especially after the positive experiences in Kosovo.

The next test facing German decision makers came two years after Kosovo in the form of the U.S.-led intervention in Afghanistan. In this chapter, I argue that at first glance, the case of Afghanistan would indeed suggest a continuation on the road to normalcy. After all, Chancellor Schröder's government – with the support of the majority of the Bundestag – promised the United States "unconditional solidarity" right from the start, including military assistance, should it become necessary. German soldiers were deployed to Afghanistan as part of "Operation Enduring Freedom" soon thereafter.

It would, however, be premature to label this an expression of a profound change in German attitudes toward the use of force in general. Afghanistan certainly does not represent a "new consensus" that should lead one to expect an increasingly assertive German foreign policy. Instead, the German participation in the mission resulted in large part from the Bundestag's perception that the lessons of history mandated German military assistance, because the United States was owed a "debt of gratitude" for its steadfast friendship since the end of World War II.

Even so, the decision to participate in the intervention could ultimately only be secured through a *Vertrauensfrage* (vote of confidence), which illustrates that Germany is far from comfortable with the use of force.

German Historical Memory of a "Special Friendship" with the United States

The terrorist attacks of September 11th, 2001, shook Germans, most of which had grown up hearing and reading about the "special friendship" between Germany and the United States. The bond between the two countries reaches back to America's war of independence, when Frederick the Great of Prussia openly sided with the American rebels by refusing to allow Hessian mercenaries, hired by England to help suppress the rebellion, to cross his territory *en route* to the colonies. Not only that, but his loyal subject Baron Friedrich Wilhelm von Steuben played a significant role in the war by organizing George Washington's army and was immortalized in American history for his contributions. The friendly relations that ensued after the war – no doubt helped along by Frederick's signing of a commercial treaty with the United States that acknowledged the principle of "free ships, free goods" – continued, mainly in the form of German emigrants seeking their fortune in the new world,[5] and in intellectual exchange visits by German scholars who wished to study American liberalism and by American scholars who attended the famous German universities.[6] During the Franco-Prussian War of 1870-71, the American Ambassador to Berlin commented on the special German-American friendship, which he said was rooted "in history and nature [because] German institutions and ours most nearly resemble each other, and because so many millions of Germans have become our countrymen."[7]

During World War I, this friendship suffered somewhat, as evidenced by the fact that German was taken off the curricula in American schools and Emperor Wilhelm was declared the "Beast of Berlin."[8] The animosity and outrage went so deep that even the Frankfurter sausages were renamed to "Liberty Sausages" so as to banish all traces of affiliation with the German enemy. Nevertheless, relations stabilized after the war before they worsened again under the Nazi regime.

After World War II, the German nation was utterly defeated, morally as well as physically. When others would have crippled the country forever with their outré demands for war reparations or their visions of a German agrarian state, only the United States' leadership realized that the former might set Germany upon the same path toward instability and extremist ideologies as it had after World War I, while the latter risked the instability of all of Europe, as a weak Germany would surely pose a target too tempting to ignore for its neighbors. By preventing such a Carthaginian peace, the United States came to be considered once again a friend of the German people, notwithstanding the fact that the U.S. actions doubtless resulted from very practical reasoning rather than a heartfelt concern for what happened to the people responsible for World War II and the Holocaust.

A deep sense of gratitude for sparing Germans, as much as could be hoped for in the wake of the war, developed, strengthened by the American practices of sending CARE packages to the starving population. Between 1946 and 1949, more than 500 million such packages were sent, each containing around 40,000 calories in the form of meat, sugar, chocolate, butter, milk, and cheese. The effect that this kind of charity had on Germans at the time should not be underestimated.[9] After an investigation revealed that in 1946, two-thirds of German children came to school without having had breakfast, it was once again the American occupiers who instituted *Schulspeisungen* (school meals), thus further reinforcing the feelings of gratitude. All in all, the way the Americans conducted themselves in the years immediately following the war anchored the image of the friendly and helpful American in Germany's collective memory.[10]

During the Cold War, the friendship was further solidified. The American aid in the form of the Marshall Plan, the assistance during the Berlin blockade of 1948-1949, and during the Berlin crisis of 1958-1962 continues to be remembered by the German people.[11] In his first speech as the Chancellor of the newly founded Federal Republic of Germany, Konrad Adenauer praised America's commitment to the political and economic reconstruction of Germany, saying that future generations would remember America more for this deed than for winning the war. In return, he said, "the German people must never, and will never, forget what the American people have done for them."[12] Fourteen years later, Adenauer's successor, Chancellor Dr. Ludwig Erhardt, also used the occasion of his first official speech to emphasize the special status the United States enjoys in the eyes of the Germans. He said that the German population "is aware of how much it has the United States to thank for, how much the freedom and security of the Federal Republic depend on the power and determination of the United States."[13]

Virtually every German leader since then has at some point or another emphasized the special nature of the transatlantic relationship, even during the Vietnam War, when anti-American protests abounded. For instance, Willy Brandt said that "the German-American friendship is irreplaceable for us"[14] and is "one of the most important realities of the international system."[15] Brandt's successor Helmut Schmidt was known for his especially good relationship with President Gerald Ford. In only three years, the two statesmen visited each other eight times. During one of Ford's visits in Germany, the German press praised him for behaving "like a U.S. tourist," participating in a boat trip along the Rhine and a dinner of Sauerkraut and beer.[16] In turn, Ford spoke very highly of Germany and Chancellor Schmidt as well: "Relations between the U.S. and West Germany were excellent throughout my Administration, primarily because Schmidt and I got along so well,"[17] he said.

In light of these frequent professions of the special friendship between Germany and the United States, it stands to reason that this particular aspect of German historical memory should play a role in the Bundestag's deliberations about the Afghanistan intervention.

German Historical Memory of Terrorism as a Social Problem

A second aspect of historical memory revolves not around World War II and its consequences, but rather around Germany's own experiences with terrorism, especially during the 1970s and 1980s. Those experiences are bound to influence the way Germans now think of terrorism in general, and of the attacks on America in particular. This assumption is based on the premise that "interpretation … is intimately and actively involved in fixing the meaning of terrorism."[18] As such, "terrorism is not so much an act as a definition of it," which is why a state's likely reaction to terrorist incidents depends more on the latter (the definition) than the former (the act itself).

Peter Merkl once wrote that "anarchism is in diametric opposition to the German mentality,"[19] which might explain why Germany – although it lacks a long history of terrorism, such as other European countries have – reacted very strongly to those few incidences that did occur. Between 1969 and 1979, Germany experienced 69 terrorist attacks on people, of which 25 resulted in death. During the same time frame there were 247 attacks involving arson and bombing, as well as 69 other serious offenses.[20] In 1980, 77 attacks were registered, followed by 129 in 1981. Compared to these numbers, Merkl said, the reaction by the German public and political system was "exaggerated and hysterical."[21]

Although Merkl was correct in his assumption that Germans dislike anarchy, he did not take into consideration that initially, there was a great deal of sympathy for the terrorists among the German population. This was perhaps due to the fact that the German brand of terrorism was mainly socially, partly politically, motivated. It occurred against the background of the students' protest movement of the 1960s in reaction to the political and social developments in the 1950s and 1960s, which were deemed unjust and unrepresentative of the ordinary man. In addition, Germans are far less patriotic than other countries' citizens tend to be. In fact, many Germans feel that it is their duty to be critical of the government – yet another remnant of the legacy of World War II – which is why there were "pockets of support"[22] for left-wing terrorism in German society; at least until people began to get killed.

A case in point is the story of Professor Peter Brückner, who took it upon himself to put his apartment in Hamburg at the disposal of Ulrike Meinhof, founding member of the (in)famous Baader-Meinhoff group, a left-wing terrorist organization in Germany. Even Nobel Prize winning author Heinrich Böll once expressed his sympathy with this group, ridiculing the government's efforts to find the terrorists by pointing out that 60 million people were hunting "a handful of young people." Böll also wrote a satire entitled "Reports on the State of Mind," an unflattering satire about the investigation of the German security services in the area of terrorism. After the murder of Federal Solicitor General Siegfried Buback by the *Rote Armee Fraktion* (RAF) in 1977, the writer of the student newspaper *Göttinger Nachrichten* commented: "My immediate reaction, my consternation, after the shooting of Buback can be quickly portrayed: I could not, did not want to (and still do not want to) conceal my furtive delight."[23]

The type of terrorism Germans have dealt with is very different from the type of terrorism the United States faced on 9/11. Walter Laqueur, considered an expert on terrorism, has made the distinction between "old" and "new" terrorism.[24] Old terrorism, which is what Germany has experienced, was mostly socially motivated. It targeted prominent figures in politics and business who were considered to be responsible for whatever ill the terrorist group wished to draw attention to. New terrorism, as displayed on September 11th, tends to be motivated by hatred and fanatical ideologies, targeting innocent civilians.

The difference in the two countries' experiences with terrorism has produced disagreement about the most efficient approach in the war against terrorism. Germans tend to think of terrorism as a social problem, an interpretation which would logically call for a "social" solution. In the past, German politicians often spoke of the need to remove the *Nährboden* (breeding grounds) for terrorism, a notion that is perfectly in line with the view of terrorism as a social problem. As such, humanitarian assistance, development aid, educational aid, and diplomacy might be considered the most appropriate tools to combat terrorism. In the United States – because of the country's own unique historical experiences with terrorism – people tend to think of terrorism as a "criminal" problem. The terrorists are portrayed as law-breakers and irrational, fanatical madmen who cannot be reasoned with and whose only goal is to cause as much damage and loss of life as possible. The logical solution that follows from such an interpretation would be to fight fire with fire, which means that a military solution would be considered the most effective approach.

With regard to the military intervention in Afghanistan, I would expect one element of historical memory – the special friendship with the United States – to contribute to Germany's willingness to participate in the mission, while the other element – German experiences with terrorism – should at least lead to disagreement about the means with which the war against terror is fought.

German National Interests in Afghanistan

Naturally, one cannot neglect the question of German national interests in the case of Afghanistan. Even without the special friendship with the United States, Germany could be expected to take the decision of whether or not to aid an ally in such a situation very seriously, despite any lingering reservations about using military force. One of the pillars of German foreign policy since 1949 had been to regain the trust of the international community and to be perceived as a reliable ally. That goal was formally expressed in a "Peace Note" the German government sent to all the countries it had diplomatic relations with in 1966. In the note is said that Germany wanted to "disperse any mistrust due to fears about aggressive intentions."[25] If the German government decided not to assist the United States in the wake of the September 11th attacks, it would potentially jeopardize its credibility as a reliable ally which it had worked so long and hard to achieve.

This is especially important because the attacks were directed against a fellow member of NATO. The importance of this alliance for German national security was already illustrated in detail in chapter 2. Article 5 of the NATO Charter states that in the event that one member is attacked, all other members will come to that member's aid. Even before the U.S. invoked Article 5 – for the first time in NATO's history – there was much speculation in the German press about this possibility and the potential consequences of such an event. Almost no one doubted that the German government would respond if called upon. The fact that this would be an out-of-area mission for the alliance had become irrelevant due to Article 5, but also because a precedent for missions outside of NATO's area of responsibility had been set with the Kosovo intervention and legalized by the German Supreme Court's decision of 1994.

Political influence, as opposed to military strength, has traditionally been the coin of German power since 1949. A country that derives its power mainly from its political influence and its economy can not afford to loose the trust of its neighbors and allies by defecting from a collective security alliance. For that reason alone, German leaders would have to seriously deliberate the advantages and disadvantages of giving military assistance in this case, despite their continued aversion to military interventions.

Other potential German interests include oil. After all, the region of Central Asia is said to hold about 10% of the world's known reserves of oil and gas. According to some reports,[26] the region's total oil reserves may reach more than 60 billion barrels of oil, which would be enough to sustain the oil needs of the European Union for a decade. The main obstacle to exploiting these oil reserves is transport. Since most of Central Asia is landlocked, pipelines would have to be laid, with the most efficient route leading through Afghanistan and Pakistan to the Arabian Sea, according to a World Bank study. In addition, Afghanistan has oil and gas reserves of its own, which make it an even more attractive target, as evidenced perhaps by Russia's 1979 invasion and the great lengths the United States went to in order to stop it.

In light of Afghanistan's geostrategic location, one could argue that Germany, which has no oil reserves of its own, has an interest in liberating Afghanistan from the oppressive regime of the Taliban in order to open up the country to German businesses and to pave the way for building an oil pipeline.

The Political Debates: "Loyal Ally Germany"

The foreign policy talk should at least partly reflect the expected thought processes outlined above: German historical memory about the special friendship with the United States, about Germany's own experience with terrorism, and German national interests – although interests still tend to not play a significant role in German foreign policy debates. And indeed, the political elites in the Bundestag did justify Germany's military participation in Operation Enduring Freedom mainly in terms of "responsibility," "solidarity," and the special relationship with America, which required Germans to repay the friendship they had experienced during the previous five decades. Figure 3.1 gives an overview of the most important themes of the debates analyzed in this chapter.

Figure 3.1: Rhetorical Map of the Afghanistan Debates

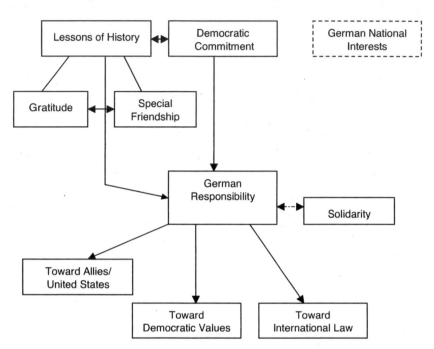

As in the case of Kosovo, the Bundestag speaker claimed that their main motivation for action had been derived from a sense of "responsibility," though – as we will see – that responsibility was interpreted somewhat differently from the previous case of Kosovo. In addition, showing "solidarity" with the United States quickly crystallized as a second theme in the speeches, closely tied to, but not synonymous, with that responsibility. Both responsibility and solidarity, however, were derived from the same sources which – as in the Kosovo debates – are the lessons of history and Germany's democratic commitment. The lessons of history in this case were very similar to the previous case, the only difference being that aspects of the World War II experience that involved the United States and its aid to Germany were the primary focus of the talk. The concept of democratic commitment also differed in some ways from the Kosovo case: while before, human rights appeared to be the most important of democratic values to be defended through a military intervention, they barely figured at all in the Afghanistan debates. Instead, other democratic values, such as freedom and peace, became the focus of most speakers. As before, German responsibility was interpreted as being a responsibility toward Germany's allies (particularly the United States), toward democratic values, and international law.

The rhetorical map in Figure 3.1 is based on the analysis of eight individual Bundestag debates. The first debate took place on September 12th, 2001, in the form of a special session of the Bundestag, during which representatives of all parties issued a public statement about the terrorist attacks. The last debate took place on December 22nd, 2001.

The Lessons of History and German Responsibility

As pointed out in earlier chapters, German experiences in WW II are frequently cited in the Bundestag debates as a source for whatever foreign policy decision is about to be made. The debates about the intervention in Afghanistan were no exception.

Michael Glos (CDU) quoted Winston Churchill as having said that "Hitler was able to become so strong, only because the democracies did not realize for a long time that great sacrifices had to be made to beat him." He used this example as a basis for appealing to the Bundestag to "let us all together be mindful of this lesson of history."

Gerhard Schröder (SPD) argued that "[i]t is a lesson of recent German history, which we have all experienced together, that pseudo-religiously motivated violence has to be overcome through democratically legitimized, external counter-violence." He added that "at the beginning of the new century, Germany is on the right side – one is tempted to say, 'finally'!" Guido Westerwelle (FDP) saw Germany's history as a positive example for the possibility of success in Afghanistan. "Just as it was possible to turn archenemies into friends in postwar Europe, it is possible to reconcile people in other regions of this earth, if the willingness and effort are large enough. That has to be the first goal of German politics."

While talk about the lessons of history is not new in Bundestag meetings, the talk in the Afghanistan debates took a special form. One of the lessons of history – as it applied to this particular situation – was that one should value one's friends and repay their friendship by showing solidarity with them. Germany had to prove itself as a good friend and ally all over again, as a direct result of the lessons of history. As Chancellor Schröder (SPD) put it, "the form of solidarity of which I have spoken is the lesson we have learned from our history. A lesson that was bitter enough for the civilized world."

The fact that it was the United States that had been attacked and required assistance made this matter even more poignant. Michael Glos (CDU), when first addressing the question of a German military contribution after the 9/11 attacks, said "[w]e Germans have experienced great friendship. In this hour of horror, we want to repay this friendship with the deepest conviction, and we have to be willing to use all means available to our country in order to help where we can." In the past, Bundestag members probably would have been much more careful to make such a general statement as "by all means necessary," because the general consensus had always been that Germany would gladly help, but certainly not by any means. During the Iraq war of 1991, all the friendship in the world could not move Germany – despite explicit appeals from the U.S. – to commit itself to more than the oft-cited "checkbook diplomacy." Now, the tone had changed.

Peter Struck (SPD) declared that "today we are all Americans." His was by far not the most dramatic declaration of friendship on that or the following days. Friedrich Merz (CDU) pointed out that "no one in the world has so much reason to show solidarity with America as we do ... especially now, we are very close to our American friends, in deep sympathy and firm friendship." He was joined by Wolfgang Gerhardt (FDP) who said he hoped that "they [the Americans] feel that – through their help in a difficult situation in the history of Germany – they have gained a great friend who firmly and committedly remains at their side."

Perhaps in the initial shock it was not surprising that the Bundestag members would impulsively declare their undying friendship. However, the friendship theme remained a constant in the entire debate, being frequently cited as a source of Germany's responsibility to show solidarity with the United States. Closely connected to the theme of a special friendship was that of German gratitude for U.S. aid after WW II. Chancellor Schröder (SPD) said that "especially in Berlin, we Germans will never forget what the United States has done for us. It was the Americans who decidedly contributed to the victory over National Socialism, and it was our American friends who made possible a new start in freedom and democracy after World War II."

German Responsibility in Afghanistan

As illustrated in the previous chapter, responsibility in general and a responsible foreign policy in particular have always been important themes in the rhetoric of the German Bundestag. This was true for this case as well.

Peter Struck (SPD) claimed that the current situation was one in which Germany was challenged to take on international responsibility. It "is not going to be easy to bear for any of us, but we must not and can not escape this responsibility." He added that it would not be enough to verbally express Germany's condolences and sympathies, but that "words have to be followed by deeds." Even early on in the debates it became clear that deeds in this case meant nothing short of participation in a military intervention, which made the seemingly ready acceptance of this type of responsibility especially interesting.

Chancellor Schröder (SPD) focused on the expectations of others for Germany to take on international responsibility in Afghanistan. "In this situation," he argued, "what is expected from Germany is active solidarity and responsible actions; a solidarity that does not only consist of words, and a foreign policy that takes into consideration Germany's responsibility in the world." German foreign policy was undergoing a transformation that began with reunification in 1990 and was slowly but surely unfolding through every new international mission Germany participated in. The intervention in Afghanistan was an important step on the way. Schröder said that "the willingness to do justice to our grown responsibility for international security means a further evolved understanding of German foreign policy. To take on international responsibility, but to avoid every immediate risk can not and must not be the guideline for German foreign and security policy." Although not all members of Schröder's coalition, or even his own party, agreed with this assessment, the fact that a German Chancellor would so openly talk about the desirability of an evolution of German foreign policy into a more assertive and militaristic one suggests that long-held taboos about Germany's role in the international system have begun to dissolve.

Angela Merkel (CDU) also argued in favor of evolution, summarizing Germany's need to take on responsibility in the most assertive language yet. She said that "these are days of horror, mourning, and anger. ... In this situation one has to know and bear one's responsibility. We have to show that we are firm and determined. Caution and insecurity must not be our course of action." Merkel had long been known for her assertiveness and her pro-American notions, so it was not surprising that she should be the one to openly call for a more confident – and ultimately more militaristic – German foreign policy. As the head of her party she expressed beliefs that were shared by many of her colleagues.

The FDP – the CDU's former coalition partner – used similar arguments that underscored the importance of German responsibility. Jürgen Koppelin (FDP) stated that "Germany has a great responsibility in foreign policy. These days have shown us that." Germany's actions had to reflect this great responsibility, as did the size and nature of Germany's contribution to international security. Koppelin used this occasion to call for a reform of Germany's defense budget, arguing that German capabilities did not match her growing international responsibility. He said that Germany's weight "is not reflected in our military budget."

Others also began to tie Germany's perceived responsibility to its capabilities for military action. Again and again the matter of the state of Germany's military surfaced in the debates, with most observers lamenting the fact that Germany – even if it wanted to take on more military responsibility – would not be capable of doing so. These complaints were nothing new in Bundestag debates. In the past 15 years, German politicians had used the lack of military capabilities time and again as a reason – one is almost tempted to say, as an excuse – to not participate in military interventions. For the first time, however, members of the Bundestag were calling for measures to remedy this problem so that in the future, Germany would be able to live up to its growing responsibilities.

Guido Westerwelle (FDP) pointed out that in addition to speaking of Germany's responsibility, "it is naturally also necessary to speak of the role of the Bundeswehr. We can not pretend that there are no problems with it." He compared the state of the Bundeswehr with a "department store in which many shelves are empty and several departments are under construction." He also called for a solution to the problem, especially if Germany was going to continue to take on more international responsibility.

Michael Glos (CDU) quoted a major German newspaper as having written that even if the Bundeswehr wanted to fight, it would not be able to. In response to this, he argued that this was an untenable situation. "Such analyses," he claimed, "must not be an excuse for Germany to take on less responsibility than others." Instead, the Bundestag would have to make sure that the Bundeswehr received the resources it needed to fulfill its role. Even more to the point, Germany's "contribution to international security must correspond to the importance of our country. That's why the role and the equipment of the Bundeswehr have to match the new situation."

Connected to Germany's responsibility was the need for solidarity with the U.S. The concepts of responsibility and solidarity in these debates were very similar in the sense that they both served as the Bundestag's main motivation for action (i.e. sending troops into Afghanistan), that they both expressed a notion of indebtedness, and that they both had the same sources, namely the lessons of history and Germany's democratic commitment.

Friedrich Merz (CDU), for instance, declared in no uncertain terms that "[w]e know where our place is. None of us would be sitting here, in the German Bundestag in Berlin, if the Americans had not shown solidarity with us Germans 50 years ago. I believe that no one in the world has as much reason to show solidarity with America as we do." Joschka Fischer (Secretary of State) did not even waste much time on justifications, merely stating that "[s]olidarity, an all-encompassing solidarity, goes without saying." Gerhard Schröder, on the other hand, explained in great detail that because of Germany's history and because of its indebtedness to the United States, solidarity was going to be expected from the Germans above any other people. "Especially we Germans," he said, "who have overcome two world wars with the help and solidarity of our American and European friends and partners in order to find freedom and self-determination, now have a duty to meet our responsibility." That responsibility was to show solidarity in return, now that the United States was the one to need it.

Different Types of Solidarity

While solidarity in general was one of the most important concepts of these debates, different types of solidarity surfaced in the speeches of the politicians over time. Initially, most speakers only referred to "solidarity," although very early on Chancellor Schröder added that Germany's solidarity would be "unconditional" or "unlimited." Most members of the Bundestag – the PDS being the notable exception – immediately adopted this term and approved an official declaration in which Germany expressed its *unconditional* solidarity with the United States. Thus the Bundestag almost from the start effectively committed itself to help the United States by any means necessary.

The PDS collectively called for a "critical solidarity," arguing that one could show solidarity with the United States, but still disagree about the means by which this war on terrorism should be fought. Not surprisingly, the PDS rejected the use of any military measures for foreign policy purposes, instead calling for a social and humanitarian approach to the fight against terrorism, claiming that since terrorism was a social problem, it should be fought with social means. Members of other parties used the term of critical solidarity as well, though not very frequently, perhaps out of fear to be associated with a party which most members of the Bundestag considered undesirable at best, and harmful at worst.

At times, speakers pointed out that not only did Germany owe solidarity out of friendship with and gratitude toward the United States, but also because of its membership in NATO. *Bündnissolidarität* (alliance solidarity) became an occasional focus of the rhetoric, expressing the overwhelming desire to prove oneself to be a reliable ally. The message this term sent was that Germany, no matter what, would stand by its allies. A word given is a word not broken.

Toward the end of the time frame analyzed here, the concept of "strategic solidarity" briefly surfaced. This kind of solidarity went beyond a limited solidarity in the current times of crisis, but formed the foundation of a future oriented partnership with the United States. Especially Chancellor Schröder used the term, perhaps implying that solidarity was not as altruistic a concept as one might assume. The word "strategic" contains the notion that an action is carefully planned, not impulsive without initial consideration of the consequences. Perhaps the Bundestag did indeed hope to gain something from showing solidarity following 9/11, rather than merely repaying the solidarity Germany had received in the past.

Solidarity Compels Action

The general consensus of the Bundestag members was that solidarity that was not followed by action was irrelevant. What was worse, it would call into question Germany's reliability and usefulness as a partner and ally, jeopardizing an important goal of German foreign policy. Thus the Bundestag's early declaration of solidarity with the U.S. effectively committed it to action, a fact which the speakers were very aware of.

Michael Glos (CDU), for instance, knew that the statement of solidarity would bring with it real consequences for German foreign policy. "In this hour of solidarity of all democracies," he said, "we want to find the firm willingness to set the necessary priorities for the security of our country, our allies, and our friends," priorities such as deploying German troops to Afghanistan. His fellow party member Friedrich Merz (CDU) added that "words have to be followed by deeds. There will be difficulties and setbacks. During the difficult times, however, true solidarity will show itself. The certain friend proves himself in uncertain times." His comment summarized the German belief that not proving itself to be a "certain friend" in times of crisis would hurt the country's image abroad. In addition, it would likely have very serious consequences for the future, as alliances are reciprocal relationships: if one member does not pull its weight, it may not receive aid in return. Or as Peter Struck (SPD) put it, "America's future international actions will be influenced by the willingness its allies show in critical times to give aid and solidarity."

Having established that the Bundestag was at least partially motivated by its perceived need to show responsibility and solidarity, derived from the lessons of history and German democratic commitment, the next logical step is to analyze which form this responsibility and solidarity took in this particular case. In the Kosovo debates, the main responsibility had been interpreted as being toward the protection of the human rights and the safety of the Kosovar-Albanian refugees. In the case of Afghanistan, the main responsibility was toward Germany's allies in general, and to the United States in particular.

Germany's Responsibility toward the United States

Germany's perceived need to prove itself a good ally has been well documented before, both by other scholars, and earlier in this book. In the current debate, this need focused on aiding the United States in what was generally considered its "darkest hour" and "time of need." In a way, German politicians almost seemed eager to have the chance to finally be the one to assist America, after having depended on American assistance for virtually all of the Federal Republic's existence.

Gerhard Schröder (SPD) declared a day after the attacks that "in this difficult hour the people of Germany stand firmly at the side of the United States of America. It goes without saying that we offer them any form of aid they wish." Dr. Ludger Volmer (Greens) stated that "we as an ally of the attacked country do not only have the moral right but the moral and political duty to aid it." Michael Glos (CDU) argued that the Bundestag needed to "send a clear signal to its allies: Germany honors its commitments." He added that "Germany has to be willing to fight against terrorism at the side of its allies, even with military means, should the Americans call for German troops."

What made the responsibility to assist the United States even more necessary was the fact that shortly after the terrorist attacks NATO for the first time invoked Article 5 of its Charter. The article is based on the idea of collective security: if one member is attacked, all members are required to assist in collective self-defense. As a result, the matter had now become what the Bundestag called a "Bündnisfall," roughly translatable as "alliance matter," though the English term does not really capture all the connotations it would contain for most Germans. Briefly put, a "Bündnisfall" is serious business, something that cannot be ignored. Not acting in such a situation is simply not an option.

Kerstin Müller (Greens) knew exactly what consequences classifying this as an "alliance matter" would have: "[by] agreeing to determine the Bündnisfall, we have encouraged the United States to act collectively and to utilize the help of its allies." Speaking for her entire party, she declared that "it was right and necessary to agree that this is a Bündnisfall. Anything else would have rendered the declarations of solidarity words without meaning." Gerhard Schröder (SPD) went even further, arguing that "our duty goes further than to merely fulfill an alliance duty ... solidarity must not be a one-way street. For decades, we have experienced solidarity. That is why it is our duty to ... give back alliance solidarity in this situation." In other words, it was not the letters of the NATO Charter that committed Germany to aid, but a moral duty that was closely connected to "Germany's identity" (Schröder), a duty to repay the aid and solidarity received.

In addition to considering it a duty, the Bundestag viewed the situation as a test of Germany's readiness to take on more international responsibility. Several members spoke of a "Bewährungsprobe" (a test of one's ability/reliability) for their country, as well as of a "Herausforderung" (challenge) that had to be met. This suggests that the basic willingness to become more active in the international arena was there; now it was necessary to prove that the capabilities matched the willingness.

Friedrich Merz (CDU) called it a "historical challenge" for Germany. "As second largest NATO-partner, population richest country in the European Union, located in the geopolitical middle of Europe," he said, "Germany has to meet its international responsibility." In order to meet this challenge, Germany would have to "prepare itself: politically, materially ... and financially." Peter Struck (SPD) claimed that "all previous challenges grow pale before the one we're facing now."

What is more, the speakers made it very clear that this would be the course of action, even if most German citizens did not agree with it. Joschka Fischer (Greens), for example, said that he was aware of the fear of the population, but that the government would have to "tell the people the bitter truth" and that it would "not be able to prevent meeting this challenge." Volker Rühe (CDU) insisted that despite the fears of the people, it was the "job of the political leadership to convince the people that this is in our country's interest."

While it became clear early on that Germany was committed to action, it was not completely decided yet what form this action should take. Article 5 of NATO's Charter does not specify the nature of assistance required from members in such a case. Theoretically, financial support or very limited military assistance, such as logistical support or granting use of airspace and German bases, would have satisfied the requirements of a *Bündnisfall*. Interestingly, almost all speakers assured the audience from the start that Germany fully intended to participate in the fight against terrorism with whatever means necessary, even if that meant the deployment of German troops into Afghanistan. Granted, Germany had come a long way since its flat-out refusal to practice anything but checkbook diplomacy in the Gulf War of 1991, but to someone who had followed the debates accompanying each deliberation of deployment of German troops throughout the 1990s, it was still somewhat surprising how quickly and openly the Bundestag members spoke of their determination to use military force in this case.

Gerhard Schröder claimed that giving military assistance was not only necessary to combat terrorism, but was also a signal for how seriously Germany took its commitments. "The willingness to secure peace with military means is an important testimony of Germany's commitment to its alliances and partnerships." Not deploying troops, then, could have called into question this commitment and perhaps led to the allies perceiving Germany as a less than equal partner. In the past, the Bundestag had not been bothered too much by such thoughts, but now the value of Germany was perceived as closely tied to its willingness to do the "dirty work" of using military force, rather than always relying on others for military security.

Joschka Fischer (Greens) stressed the need for a military response by pointing out that perhaps a military answer to the World Trade Center attacks in 1993 would have been able to prevent 9/11. He said that the "United States reacted by arresting those involved and trying them in court. All that did not prevent September 11th." He added that "as terrible as it is, there is such a thing as realist consequences of pacifist actions. We cannot use humanitarian interventions everywhere." Instead, Germany would not be able to avoid "using the necessary military means."

Friedrich Merz (CDU) claimed that the option to not use military force simply did not exist. As difficult as it would be, he said, "there will be military actions, there will have to be." Dr. Wolfgang Gerhardt (FDP) made the same argument, adding that even though many Germans did not believe in military solutions, this situation clearly called for one. He said that despite all other efforts, Germany "would not be able to avoid the use of military means, against people who – despite the popular idealism of Germans – simply cannot be reformed." And according to Peter Struck (SPD), Germany "needs the willingness to participate in this fight with military means, if necessary."

Germany's Responsibility to Uphold Democratic Values

In addition to the responsibility to aid Germany's allies, the Bundestag recognized the responsibility to act on the basis of democratic values. As pointed out before, the Bundestag takes Germany's democratic commitment very seriously, and although in the past a passive adherence to democratic values had been enough, the new self-understanding of Germany as a democratic power included the active defense of those values abroad, should the need arise. In the case of Kosovo, the defense of democratic values had focused on the protection of human rights above any other value. In the case of Afghanistan, human rights did not figure as prominently in the rhetoric of the Bundestag members as only two years before. Instead, other values – also closely associated with being a democracy – received the main attention

As a democracy, Germany was part of the "civilized" world whom, in the Bundestag's interpretation of the matter, the terrorist attacks had been directed against. Because of that, Germany could not afford to stand aside and let others such as the United States take care of the problem. Instead, Germany had to make its contribution in the defense of democratic values in the world. Dr. Guido Westerwelle (FDP) made this point when he said that Germany's allies expect "our contribution to secure peace and freedom in the world. All democracies have this great responsibility." He also discounted a pacifist response, stating that "one can not secure peace and freedom with protests. Now it is essential that we become a *wehrhafte Demokratie* [a democracy that defends itself]. Just as we defend democracy internally, we have to do so externally; otherwise we jeopardize the roots of who we are."

Heidemarie Wieczorek-Zeul (SPD) also considered the defense of democratic values one of the important tasks of German foreign policy in the future: we have to "improve the prospects for peace, justice, and solidarity for all. This is the great task of our generation and the one that will follow us. I say: we will take this responsibility seriously."

Gerhard Schröder repeatedly tied the defense of these values to Germany's self-understanding as a state. Since German identity was based on democratic values, it followed that if these values were attacked, it was also an attack on everything the country stood for. "This type of terrorist violence," he said, "this random extinction of innocent lives, questions the basic rules of our civilization. It immediately threatens the principles of living together in freedom and security, everything which has been accomplished in generations. Together ... we will not allow these values to be destroyed ... These values are our identity, and that is why we will defend them."

The members of the Bundestag were aware that many Germans remained highly skeptical of military interventions and would probably prefer to fight terrorism by other, peaceful means. In response, many of the speakers pointed out that in some situations, the defense of democratic values would require Germans to overcome their fears and to do what must be done. Michael Glos (CDU) claimed that "Fear is a bad advisor. The best thing we can do for a safe life in peace and freedom is to extinguish terrorism once and for all."

This talk about the defense of democratic values, if necessary with military means, clearly illustrates the change in German foreign policy rhetoric toward a more assertive and more active policy. Germany's new responsibility included the willingness to deploy German troops in order to fulfill its duty, underlining how serious Germany was about this new course.

Germany's Responsibility toward International Law

A third dimension of German responsibility in the political rhetoric was that of a responsibility to uphold international law. In the Kosovo debates, international law had played a very large role in the Bundestag rhetoric. In the Afghanistan debates, that was not the case, at least judging from the frequency counts alone. However, just because international law was not a dominant topic of conversation, that does not mean that Germany did not consider it part of its responsibility. When looking at the instances in which speakers did address international law, it became clear that it remained an important aspect of German foreign policy to adhere to and to defend international law. From a legal perspective, the intervention in Afghanistan was much less questionable than the intervention in Kosovo for several reasons. Firstly, NATO had invoked Article 5 of its Charter, giving the mission an official character. Secondly, the United Nations Charter explicitly allows the use of military force in self-defense, which was presumably what the United States could claim with regard to Afghanistan. Thirdly, the United Nations had passed previous resolutions that specifically authorized the intervention in Afghanistan. The fact that the mission – and Germany's participation in it – rested on a firm legal basis likely rendered long discussions about international law unnecessary.

Nonetheless, the members of the Bundestag were happy to point out that this legal basis indeed did exist. Gerhard Schröder (SPD) reported that "the Security Council of the United Nations has determined in Resolution 1368 that the terrorist attacks ... represent a threat to world peace and international security ... thus the legal prerequisites for a

decisive, military intervention against terrorism are met." Friedrich
Merz (CDU) commented on how quickly the United Nations had made
that decision, saying that "the Security Council of the United Nations
has never before made such a decision as quickly and clearly as it did in
this case." Even the representative of the traditionally pacifist Green
Party conceded that "of course the United States has the legitimate right
to defend itself, according to international law" (Kerstin Müller).
Michael Glos (CDU) pointed out that the military reaction to the
terrorist attacks was covered from two legal angles: "The NATO-council
has unanimously invoked Article 5 of the Charter and the Security
Council of the United Nations has backed these measures and separately
called for the punishment of the perpetrators and supporters."

Because the terrorists were the ones who have violated international
law, the United States and its allies not only had the right to punish
them, but had the responsibility to do so, according to the speakers in the
Bundestag.

German National Interests

In the past, any talk of German interests had been notably absent from
Bundestag debates, especially in cases of foreign policy decisions that
included the potential deployment of military troops.[27] It was almost as
though German leaders were afraid that hearing the terms "German
military" and "German interests" in the same context would send all of
Europe into a state of panic, expecting German soldiers to pour across
the border by the thousands in order to make yet another bid at German
hegemony. It is questionable how many of Germany's neighbors still
associate the German army of the year 2000 with those of 1914 and
1938, but it is relatively certain that for many German politicians, this
remains a sensitive issue. As a result, whenever the talk centered on the
use of the Bundeswehr, German leaders tended to be especially careful
about their choice of words, perhaps in order to reassure their foreign –
and domestic – audiences. In the case of Kosovo, the term "German
interests" was mentioned only fourteen times in six long debates;
instead, the members of the Bundestag argued that German military
participation was not a matter of national interest, but rather a
"humanitarian responsibility."

Before this background, it was a little surprising that in the
Afghanistan debates, German interests actually played a role. Or to be
more specific – as they surely played a role in the Kosovo case as well –
that they were actually *talked* about openly. Granted, the rhetoric used
creates the impression that a sense of responsibility and solidarity was

the driving force behind Germany's decision to participate in the military intervention in Afghanistan, but the fact that German interests would be brought up at all suggests that perhaps the Bundestag members had lost some of their reluctance to claim the same right for their country as any other country's representatives would, namely to not only act in their best interest, but to admit that this was so.

Of those interests addressed in the debates, the one that stood out above any other was that of "security." Many of the speakers argued that even though they primarily approved of the military intervention because of Germany's responsibility in the world and toward its friends and allies, a secondary concern revolved around German national security. As the terrorist attacks were interpreted as directed against not only the United States, but against the entire civilized world, the speakers pointed out that it was also in Germany's "Eigeninteresse" (own interest) to contribute to the fight against terrorism.

Peter Struck (SPD), for example, said that because of the universal threat of terrorism – it could strike anyone at any time – it "is not only our duty as an ally to fight international terrorism with our American friends and NATO partners, but it is a matter of our very own interest." Rezzo Schlauch (Bündnis 90/Die Grünen) encouraged the Bundestag to derive from this situation "the firm will to set the necessary priorities for the security of our country."

It was interesting to see how far the debate about German security went. Several members – in a debate that was not included in this analysis because it focused exclusively on domestic responses to the terrorist threat – called for a new law that would allow the Bundeswehr to carry out certain domestic police duties in case of a crisis. In other countries, this practice was neither new nor controversial, but in light of Germany's World War II experiences, such a step had been considered out of the question thus far. The thought of uniformed soldiers patrolling the streets of German cities left too many uneasy to seriously consider the possibility. Up until now! The calls for a reform in order to allow just that were rejected before ever being turned into a proposal. Nonetheless, the fact that a serious debate about the matter had even been opened up in the Bundestag may suggest that yet another taboo connected to German World War II experiences could soon be crumbling.

Despite the increased frequency with which Bundestag members spoke of German interests, a closer look at the way they phrased this talk suggests that there remained some reluctance or uneasiness accompanying such talk. Rudolf Scharping (Secretary of Defense), for instance, said that military action was in Germany's "interest as a liberal democracy." Thus he implied that these were not uniquely German interests that motivated the decision, but interests that were shared by all democracies interested in promoting freedom around the world. Put that way, talk of German interests sounded much less frightening than it had the potential to.

Gert Weisskirchen (SPD) employed a similar rhetorical strategy by saying that it "lies in the interest of all peoples, including the Federal Republic of Germany's, to fight terrorism worldwide." Volker Rühe (CDU) also generalized German interests. He said, "That is why fighting terrorism is in all our interests," whereby "all our" could refer to the interests of all Germans or the interests of all democracies.

By placing German interests into the much larger context of Europe, democracies in general, or even the entire "civilized world," the speakers were trying to reassure their audiences that despite once again speaking of German interests, Germany considered itself part of a lager community and would only pursue its interests within the perimeters of that community. This was a strategy that German leaders had been employing for decades.

In addition to national security, a secondary German interest that surfaced often in the debates stemmed from concerns about the influx of foreigners into Germany. Debates about immigration had been a notoriously sensitive issue, as Germans did not want to be perceived as xenophobic because they were restricting immigration into the country.

Interestingly, many of the politicians now spoke of German interests with regard to the restriction of immigration. In the case of Kosovo, the refusal to allow more Albanian refugees into the country had been justified not by pointing to interests, but by arguing that keeping the refugees close to their homes by erecting refugee camps in Macedonia was ultimately in the best interest of the refugees themselves. Gerhard Schröder – as he appears to do so often – took the lead in the Afghanistan debates as well, arguing that "as the land in the middle of Europe, we have a considerable interest in deciding a regulation of immigration that is feasible in the future."

Perhaps German leaders were less afraid of using interest-based language in their call for new immigration laws, because they could expect a certain amount of understanding for such measures, considering that the 9/11 attacks had been carried out by immigrants and other countries were reconsidering their own immigration laws as well[28].

Ultimately there were two different explanations for the more frequent usage of interest-based talk in this case: either German politicians had only just begun to care about German interests in their foreign policy decision making, or they had pursued German interests all along, but merely felt they could not talk about them openly for fear of arousing suspicion. As a completely interest-free foreign policy of any country is too utopian to imagine, it is probably the latter explanation that applies here.

Nonetheless, the fact that German interests are being talked about again constitutes an interesting finding in and of itself, as it may be a sign that the generation that felt the need to disguise German interests with talk of more altruistic motives is slowly dying out. In that case, we might expect this trend to continue until eventually Germany will behave as any other "normal" nation would, both in words and deeds. One of the questions to be answered later on will be to what degree this change has already happened, i.e. how strong of a hold the restrictions the World War II experience has placed on German foreign policy still have on the minds of German decision makers.

Talk about Action

When discussing the type of action to be taken, the main focus in the debates was on a military versus a political solution to the problem. In the past, the Bundestag had almost always preferred a political solution that focused on diplomacy, humanitarian aid, and development aid. In this case, almost every speaker – with the exception of members of the PDS and a few members of the Green Party – agreed that a military solution may not be the most desirable solution, but definitely necessary.

At the same time, the majority felt the need to point out that even though a military action was the first step to solving this problem, it could by no means be the only one. Instead, a quick military intervention was supposed to pave the way for a political solution that would create a lasting peace. Here the different perceptions of terrorism in Germany, as opposed to the United States, might have come into play. Based on Germany's own experiences with terrorism, i.e. with a type of terrorism that was motivated by social goals and usually directed against the upper class, most members of the Bundestag interpreted the problem as a social one. In other words, poverty, inequality, and injustice were considered to be the *Nährboden* (breeding ground) for terrorism.

Because that was the case, a strictly military response to what was a political and social problem would be bound to fail. That explains why almost every time a Bundestag member advocated a military intervention, that statement was followed by the qualification that the response had to go beyond just the military aspect in order to focus on a comprehensive solution that incorporated military, political, and humanitarian means.

A "Turning Point" in German Foreign Policy?

Another finding that is of interest with regard to the future of German foreign policy is that many of the speakers interpreted the Afghanistan case as a "turning point" of some sort. Joschka Fischer (Greens) said so in connection with talks about the future budget for Germany's foreign policy: "The terrorist attacks were a turning point. ... When we talk about the budget, we cannot ignore the totally new orientation we were forced to adopt." Kerstin Müller (Bündnis 90/Die Grünen) agreed with her party leader, saying that "we all feel that in the past weeks something has fundamentally changed. This is a political turning point after which nothing will be as it was." Angela Merkel (CDU) addressed the implications such a turning point would have for Germany's future: "September 11th," she said, "was a turning point. Today we are for the first time deliberating what consequences this will have. We are facing very real consequences economically, politically, diplomatically, and – I'm adding this very explicitly – militarily." Dr. Guido Westerwelle (FDP) even called it a "historical turning point for German foreign and security policy."

It remains to be seen exactly what – if any – changes in German foreign policy will result from this turning point in the future. The next chapter on the war against Iraq will certainly be a starting point for analyzing any potential changes.

Some Differences in the Rhetoric

Once again the debates exhibited a great deal of consensus across party lines, at least in their rhetoric. Despite some grumbling, all parties except the PDS expressed their support for the government's course of action in Afghanistan. Or as Guido Westerwelle (FDP) put it: "In the joint fight against terrorism and in the matter of the inner and outer security there can be no argument between parties. Germany deserves a responsibility across party lines." The extraordinary circumstances of the decision certainly added to the perception that there never was a genuine choice in the matter. During the initial phase of shock, most members of the Bundestag had promised the United States solidarity in some form, even the members of the PDS, thus committing Germany to action. After NATO's Article 5 was invoked, the Bundestag felt it had even less of a choice.

As might have been expected, the government coalition addressed the issue of security much more often than any other party. It would naturally fall to the parties in power to reassure the German public that their elected representatives would do all in their power to ensure their safety. In addition, members of the government also debated the legality of the Afghanistan mission in much greater detail than did the other parties, primarily emphasizing that this was a multilateral mission, that it was lawful and moral, and that there was a United Nations mandate for it. This made sense as well, because if the intervention had been perceived as illegal, then the government likely would have been blamed, not the opposition. Therefore the members of the SPD and the Greens had an interest in establishing legitimacy for the German participation from the beginning. The only other party that spoke fairly frequently of legal issues was the PDS. In contrast to the government's rhetoric, however, the members of the PDS claimed that Germany was violating international law by engaging in an out-of-area mission in Afghanistan.

Foreign Policy Rhetoric: Male vs. Female Speakers
Whereas in the Kosovo debates a meaningful analysis of the difference in rhetoric between male and female members of the Bundestag was not feasible due to the lack of female speakers, the Afghanistan debates did allow for such a comparison. Table 3.1 summarizes the number of female representatives in the 14th Bundestag across parties.

Traditionally, the Green Party (57.4%) and the PDS (58.3%) are the two parties with the largest percentage of women, mainly due to their policies that effectively ensure equal representation for women. The CDU (18.4%) and the FDP (20.9%) traditionally have the lowest numbers of female members, while the SPD (35.2%) is somewhere in the middle. In part, these percentages reflect the fact that women tend to hold views that are more in line with the platforms of the center-left (SPD, Greens) and far-left (PDS) parties than the platforms of the center-right (CDU, FDP) or far-right (not represented). In all, there were eight female speakers, constituting 7.3% of the total number of speakers. Compared to the numbers in Table 3.1, the percentage of female speakers is unfortunately not at all representative of their numbers in the Bundestag, so the findings discussed below should be viewed with the proper caution. It should also be kept in mind that many of the women represented the Greens and the PDS, both known for their pacifist tendencies.

In general, the female speakers tended to speak more about the legality of the intervention in Afghanistan, in particular the need for multilateralism as a means to lend the mission legitimacy: only 7.3% of the speakers accounted for 23.2% of the total number of instances in which multilateralism was addressed. In addition, the women spoke more about the role of the United Nations (22% of the total number),

international law (21%), and the rule of law in general (21.7%).
Interestingly, though perhaps not surprisingly, the women also focused
more on the importance of humanitarian aid (18.4% of total) and human
rights (27%). It was clear that in general, the female speakers would
have preferred a non-violent solution to the problem. At the same time,
the women emphasized the importance of security (20.4%) much more
than their male counterparts, at least proportionately, and considered
terrorism much more of a threat (22.2%). They tended to speak much
less of interests (8.4% of total), defense (11.5%), the European Union
(8.7%), and the United States (4.8%).

Table 3.1 Women in the 14th German Bundestag (1998-2002)			
Party	Women	Total	Percentage
CDU	45	245	18.4 %
SPD	105	298	35.2 %
Greens	27	47	57.4 %
FDP	9	43	20.9 %
PDS	21	36	58.3 %
Total	207	669	30.9 %

Foreign Policy Rhetoric: "Young" vs. "Old"
The 14th Bundestag, which was in session from 1998 until 2002, looked
significantly "younger" than the previous one, as shown in Table 3.2.
Whereas in the 13th Bundestag (1994-1998) only 23.5% of all members
had been born after 1950, that number had increased to 33% in the 14th
Bundestag. The number of representatives who had been born before
1935 decreased from 10.9% in the 13th Bundestag to only 3.4% in the
14th Bundestag. While it is rare for younger members to have the chance
to speak before the parliament, the age make-up of the body as a whole
might have an effect on the perception of historical memory in the
debates.

Based on those who did address the Bundestag in the Afghanistan
debates, the younger speakers, who were born after 1950, were generally
much less reluctant to speak about Germany's national interests than the
older speakers – they accounted for roughly 36% of all instances in
which interests were addressed –, even though the total number still

paled compared to other, more idealist rhetoric. Simultaneously, these speakers were also more concerned about Germany's security, accounting for almost 60% of all instances. This suggests that a certain generational effect is at work here. Unlike the older generations, these speakers do not appear constrained by the memories of World War II, at least not to a point where it prevents them from talking about national interests and national security.

Table 3.2: Age Divisions of the 14th German Bundestag (1998-2002)													
	Men						Women						
Birth Year	CDU	SPD	GR	FDP	PDS	total	CDU	SPD	GR	FDP	PDS	total	BT total
1926-1930	1	3	-	-	1	5	-	-	-	-	-	-	5
1931-1935	4	9	1	-	2	16	1	1	-	-	-	2	18
1936-1940	33	37	1	7	1	79	17	6	-	-	1	24	103
1941-1045	63	56	-	13	2	134	25	8	2	1	2	38	172
1946-1950	40	39	6	8	4	97	27	13	6	3	4	53	150
1951-1955	25	27	6	3	3	64	17	7	8	3	4	39	103
1956-1960	11	17	2	1	1	32	9	3	5	1	5	23	55
1961-1965	9	10	1	2	-	22	4	3	2	1	3	13	35
1966-1970	5	2	-	-	1	8	5	3	3	-	-	11	19
1971-1975	1	-	3	-	-	4	-	1	1	-	2	4	8
1976-1980	1	-	-	-	-	1	-	-	-	-	-	-	1
Total	193	200	20	34	15	462	105	45	27	9	21	207	669

Source: German Bundestag, 2006
BT = Bundestag
CDU = Christian Democratic Union
FDP = Free Democratic Party
GR = Greens
SPD = Social Democratic Party
PDS = Party of Democratic Socialism

Another sign for a more independent way of thinking among the younger speakers is how rarely they spoke about NATO, the United States, and "gratitude" compared to the rest of the Bundestag speakers. The North Atlantic Treaty Organization as a Cold War alliance had perhaps lost some of its importance in the minds of younger generations of Germans. In contrast, the older speakers had always insisted on the importance of the alliance for German security. In Kosovo, the need to support NATO had been one of the most frequently talked about motivation for Germany's military participation. Even in the Afghanistan debates, NATO continued to play an important role. Since the Bundestag was still primarily run by the older generation at that point, one has to wonder what will happen in another decade or so, when the younger members will have taken over more responsibility and decision making power.

The same is true for the special friendship with the United States in connection with German gratitude. The younger speakers talked much less frequently of the United States, even though the majority of the Bundestag made America the primary focus of the debates. Even more importantly, the younger generation did not appear to share the same sense of gratitude, which their elders had cited as one of the motivations for action. This may not bode well for the future of the German-American relationship.

Interestingly, even though the younger speakers may not have shared the same historical memories with the older generation, their rhetoric was still influenced by the notions of responsibility and solidarity. Though they may not have been derived from the same sources, they certainly continued to play a role in the younger generation's thought processes as expressed in their speeches. The same was true for other lessons of history: the younger speakers were just as, if not more, likely to bring up German history in their speeches as the rest of the Bundestag, with the only difference that the lessons they drew from it were slightly different.

German Troops at the Hindu Kush:
A Special Type of Solidarity

Despite the relative peacefulness and agreement during the debates, all did not end well in the German Bundestag when it came to the actual decision of sending 3,900 Bundeswehr troops into Afghanistan. Perhaps the rhetoric was slightly deceiving, because only the most prominent members of the various parties actually got to speak in front of the assembly; they were naturally expressing the official party line. Others, especially members of the formerly and perhaps yet again pacifist Green Party, may not have gotten their chance in the Bundestag meetings, but were not shy about expressing their disapproval in newspapers and talk shows, or, for that matter, about expressing their intent to vote against the mission, thus endangering the entire plan despite their leading men and women's verbal commitments to deploy German troops in the debates.

Ultimately, Chancellor Schröder had to tie the decision to a vote of confidence. Afraid that a negative vote would now mean an end not only to the unwelcome Bundeswehr mission, but also to their own, very welcome seat in the Bundestag, the majority of dissenters selflessly put their moral concerns aside and voted "yes" on both accounts. In the end, the vote of confidence — and therefore the vote to deploy troops – was supported by 336 to 326 votes.[29] More than 70 members of the Greens attached a written explanation to their vote in parliament, stating that they had voted in favor of the mission only in order to preserve the stability of the German government. A handful of dissenters were allowed to symbolically express their moral, but now utterly inconsequential, pacifist concerns in the Bundestag.

This internal disagreement over the decision to deploy troops was the result of a few factors. Firstly, many Bundestag members remained somewhat skeptical about the U.S.-led war on terrorism. In particular, Germans feared American unilateralism down the road and were concerned about George W. Bush's increasingly black-and-white rhetoric. Only the initial promise of solidarity and the historical memory of the friendship between the two countries were able to produce enough support for the mission. The fact that this special friendship may be waning implies that in the future, this support may not be as forthcoming. The vote also revealed that the belief in antimilitarism was not quite a thing of the past yet. Especially the members of the Greens did not feel very comfortable with the Afghanistan mission. Their loyalty in this matter was highly conditional, which also holds serious implications for the future of German foreign policy.

A Return to German Militarism?

At a first glance, the rhetoric employed in the Afghanistan debates appeared to be very similar to the one employed in the Kosovo debates. In both cases – as in every other case involving the possibility of German participation in a military intervention in the 1990s – responsibility was cited as the foremost motivation for action or inaction. Germany appeared to be committed to practice a "responsible" foreign policy, but exactly what that means was open to interpretation. During the early 1990s, it was Germany's responsibility to never send German soldiers into areas where the Nazis had committed such atrocities during World War II. Chancellor Kohl made that argument in the early 1990s when Germany had been asked to participate in a peacekeeping mission in Bosnia. In 1999, Germany's responsibility was interpreted as sending German soldiers into the Balkans in order to protect human rights. In 2001, the protection of human rights became secondary to offering solidarity and friendship (along with military assistance) to the United States in its fight against terrorism. Although Germany had not been practicing a completely erratic foreign policy and most of its actions could indeed be described as at least attempting to be responsible, it also became clear that there was some leeway in the interpretation of what exactly that responsibility entailed and whom it was owed to.

In both cases analyzed thus far, the lessons of history and Germany's democratic commitment were quoted as being the source of German foreign policy, specifically of Germany's duty to act responsibly. However, the lessons learned from the World War II experience and the different aspects of being a committed democracy were quite numerous. It almost seemed as though there was a lesson for every occasion, and a particular democratic duty for every situation Germany has ever found itself in. Presumably, World War II taught Germans to *always* stand up for human rights and to protect them. However, during the early 1990s, it appeared to be enough to not cause any human rights violations, while in Kosovo, it suddenly became necessary to defend the human rights of the Kosovar-Albanians. In Afghanistan, the human rights of the Afghan population became secondary to the objective of fighting terrorism and aiding a "special" friend. In this case, the lesson learned from World War II was that Germany had a responsibility to repay the friendship and solidarity it received from the United States.

The question this raises is whether Germany's talk of responsibility, the lessons of history, and democratic commitment is perhaps more of a "template" that gives rough guidelines for the conduct of German foreign policy, while the details can be filled in on a case-to-case basis.

More Assertive Language

Foreign policy rhetoric in the Afghanistan debates had become much more assertive than in the Kosovo debates. In addition to the fact that speakers talked more freely about German interests, there were other noteworthy words and phrases that indicated a change in the rhetoric used. For example, whereas a "level-headed" foreign policy used to be praised as the ultimate way to carry on international relations, now German leaders were calling for a "determined" foreign policy with "firmness" and "strength." Whereas being a "democracy" whose citizens lived in accordance with democratic values used to be considered good policy, now the term of "a democracy that defends itself" (*wehrhafte Demokratie*) was slowly taking that place, implying that the time had come to not only passively obey the rules, but actively ensure that others did so as well. Whereas the motto used to be "to never cause any harm," the new motto was "to not stand by and watch others cause harm." Yet another favorite concept of German foreign policy, namely *Friedenspolitik* (peace policy), appeared to be undergoing a transformation in meaning as well. Whereas it used to be interpreted as "practicing a peaceful policy," it could now be more adequately described as "practicing a policy that defends peace."

The change in the rhetoric could indicate a change in the way Germans think about their role in the international system, specifically about participating in military missions abroad.

German Salami Tactics?

The topic of deploying troops to Afghanistan for purposes other than humanitarian assistance was not as sensitive as may have been expected. In the Kosovo debates, most speakers approved the deployment of the Bundeswehr, but were very careful to constantly remind audiences that German soldiers were only going to use force to defend themselves and otherwise carry out a strictly humanitarian mission in order to help the Kosovar-Albanians. In the Afghanistan debates, quite a few speakers used very frank words about the military nature of this mission. In combination with the more frequently used realist language and the mentioning of German interests, this may suggest an evolution of German thinking with regard to the use of the Bundeswehr as a foreign policy tool and the type of missions considered appropriate. Perhaps Germany is indeed engaging in "salami tactics," i.e. slowly getting domestic and foreign audiences used to the idea of a more assertive German foreign policy. Certainly the talks about the reform of the Bundeswehr indicate that some changes might be expected.

How Genuine Is the German-American Friendship in the 21st Century?

How Genuine Is the German-American Friendship in the 21st Century?

Much was made of the special nature of the German-American friendship in the Afghanistan debates, yet one can not help but wonder exactly how "special" this friendship still is, or ever was, for that matter. In the beginning, when Adenauer and his successors proclaimed everlasting friendship, Germany really was not an equal by any stretch of the imagination, making the relationship with the United States somewhat one-sided. It was probably not exactly friendship the Americans were feeling for the newly defeated Germany, either. The latter may have felt relief and some gratitude, but perhaps friendship is also too strong of a word; cynics might call it a euphemism for dependence. Throughout the Cold War, perhaps a kind of friendship developed between the two countries, but it would be hard to say how genuine it was considering the continued dependence of Germany on the United States for security and the continued U.S. occupation of German territory.

Dependence, unfortunately, often does not end in everlasting gratitude and friendship, but rather breeds resentment.[30] The German leadership does not often openly criticize the United States, but the German people usually have no such reservation, as the mass protests during the 1991 Gulf War showed. Since then, many observers have commented on a latent anti-Americanism in Germany, not only among the population, but increasingly among the leadership as well. Chancellor Schröder certainly does not appear too inhibited by feelings of friendship and gratitude. While in power, he frequently practiced a – for German standards – rather independent foreign policy, such as when he deepened relations with China and Russia despite misgivings across the Atlantic. All in all, a certain erosion of German-American friendship over the last decade can not be denied. "The older generation of Atlanticists is stepping aside on both sides," as one scholar observed in the mid-1990s.[31]

In the Afghanistan debates, there were critical comments as well, despite the official declarations of solidarity and friendship. One speaker perceived Germans to be "prisoners of the situation," while another said that "either we do this voluntarily, or the Americans will put immense pressure on us." Even though voices like these were in the minority in the Bundestag, it stands to reason that they expressed what many were thinking but not willing to say. If that were true, it would call into question the depth of the German-American friendship. It also makes one wonder what would happen if Germany ever had to choose between its European and its American friends.

---

[1] Kai Erikson (1966). Wayward Puritans: A Study in the Sociology of Deviance. New York, NY: Wiley.

[2] Scott Erb (2003). German Foreign Policy: Navigating a New Era. Boulder, CO: Lynne Rienner Publishers; Gunther Hellmann (1999). "Nationale Normalität als Zukunft? Zur Außenpolitik der Berliner Republik," Blätter für deutsche und international Politik, vol. 44, no. 7, pp. 837-47; Werner Reutter, ed., (2004). Germany on the Road to 'Normalcy': Policies and Politics of the Red-Green Federal Government (1998-2002)." New York, NY: Palgrave, Macmillan; August Pradetto (2004). "From 'Tamed' to 'Normal' Power: A New Paradigm in German Foreign and Security Policy?" in: Reutter, ed., Germany on the Road to 'Normalcy,' pp. 209-235; E. Bahr (1999). "Die 'Normalisierung' der deutschen Außenpolitik: Mündige Partnerschaft statt bequemer Vormundschaft," Internationale Politik, vol 54, no. 1, pp. 41-52.

[3] Scott Erb (2003). German Foreign Policy: Navigating a New Era, p. 167.

[4] Newsweek, April 1999.

[5] Between 1820 and 1970, almost seven million Germans immigrated into the United States; today, more than 60 million Americans can look back on German ancestors.

[6] Between 1830 and 1870, no less than 12,000 young Americans attended German universities in hope of receiving their Ph.D. there. Many American universities were in fact modeled after the German educational system.

[7] Quoted in: Manfred Jonas (1984). The United States and Germany. Ithaca, NY: Cornell University Press.

[8] Graf Johann-Heinrich von Bernstorff (1920). Deutschland und Amerika: Erinnerungen aus dem fünfjährigen Kriege. Berlin.

[9] My own grandmother insisted on sending packages of chocolate, candy, and socks to American soldiers in Bosnia in the mid-1990s, because – as she said – "it only seems right, because they sent us food after the war."

[10] See Rainer Gries (1991). Die Rationen-Gesellschaft: Versorgungskampf und Vergleichmentalität. Leipzig, pp. 210-13; Hermann Glaser (1991). Kleine Kulturgeschichte der Bundesrepublik Deutschland 1945-1989. Bonn, p. 62 f.; Theodor Eschenburg (1983). Jahre der Besatzung 1945-1949. Stuttgart, pp. 396-99.

[11] Former President Richard von Weizsäcker, for instance, honored the role of the Americans during those times in his famous speech of May 8th, 1985, on the occasion of the 40th anniversary of the end of World War II.

[12] Konrad Adenauer, First Government Statement, delivered on September 20, 1949, in: Außenpolitik der Bundesrepublik Deutschland: Dokumente von 1949 bis 1994, pp. 170-175.

[13] Dr. Ludwig Erhardt, First Government Statement, delivered on October 18, 1963; in: ibid., pp. 281-83.

[14] Willy Brandt in a speech delivered before the VI. German American Conference, January 24th, 1970, in: Presse- und Informationsamt der

Bundesregierung, ed., (1973) Bundeskanzler Brandt: Reden und Interviews. Bonn, p. 116.

[15] Willy Brandt in a speech delivered at the White House, April 10, 1970, in: Bundeskanzler Brandt: Reden, p. 175.

[16] "Ford macht Station in Bonn," Süddeutsche Zeitung, July 17, 1975; "Mit Bier und Wein und Sauerkraut," Frankfurter Allgemeine Zeitung, July 29th, 1975.

[17] Gerald Ford (1979). A Time to Heal. New York.

[18] Annamarie Oliverio (1998). The State of Terror. Albany, NY: State University of New York Press, pp. 18-19.

[19] Peter Merkl (1986). Political Violence and Terror. Berkley, CA: University of California Press, p. 191.

[20] Friedhelm Neidhardt (1982). "Linker und rechter Terrorismus. Erscheinungsformen und Hand-

lungspotentiale im Gruppenvergleich," in: Wanda von Baeyer-Katte et al., Gruppenprozesse. Opladen: Westdeutscher Verlag, pp. 433-476.

[21] Merkl, Political Violence and Terror, p. 192.

[22] Hans Joseph Horchem (1991). "The Terrorist Lobby in Germany: Campaigns and Propaganda in Support of Terrorism," in: Noemi Gal-Or, ed., Tolerating Terrorism in the West: An International Survey. New York: Routledge.

[23] Quoted in: Naomi Gal-Or, ed., Tolerating Terrorism in the West: An International Survey. New York: Routledge, p. 151.

[24] See Walter Laqueur (1999). The New Terrorism: Fanaticism and the Arms of Mass Destruction. New York, NY: Oxford University Press.

[25] Friedensnote der Bundesregierung, March 25, 1966; in: Außenpolitik der Bundesrepublik Deutschland, p. 295-299.

[26] See Union Oil Company of California (UNOCAL).

[27] Interestingly, this reluctance to speak of German interests does not appear to extend to economic matters, although a systematic analysis of debates in that area is beyond the scope of this work. In addition, German leaders seem to be fairly comfortable speaking of collective "European" interests, even when those interests could be interpreted as benefiting Germany more so than other members of the EU.

[28] For instance, Great Britain, France, and Denmark reformed their immigration laws after the September 11, 2001, terrorist attacks.

[29] Naturally, the members of the government opposition all voted "no" on the measure, not because they opposed the deployment of German troops, but because they hoped the vote of confidence would fail and thus pave the way for new elections.

[30] See Dirk Verheyen (1999). The German Question: A Cultural, Historical, and Geopolitical Exploration. Boulder, CO: Westview Press.

[31] Cord Jakobeit (1996). The United States and German-American Relations through German Eyes, Commack, NY: Nova Science Publishers, pp. 31-32.

4

Defender of Peace and of the United Nations: The Case of Iraq

"Am deutschen Wesen soll die Welt genesen."[1]
(Let the German essence heal the world)
— German Imperial Adage

"Our Germany trusts in its own strength.
Our Germany is a confident country.
Our Germany enjoys respect in the world,
because we are partners and shining example.
Because we are building the Europe of people
and protecting peace and human rights worldwide.
And because we do not have to hide our national interests.
That is our German way." — Gerhard Schröder, August 2002

Throughout the Federal Republic's fifty-year history, the idea of a "German way" had been feared and avoided as an expression of nationalist aspirations. Whenever Germany had been left alone in the past, its path had invariably led it "away from the values of the West, toward a rejuvenation of German nationalism, with its attendant specter of aggression and war."[2] In the aftermath of World War II – the latest of Germany's special paths – the victorious powers decided that the only way to prevent future German unilateralist aspirations was to bind the land of the middle to a system of other nations. Thus the idea that would ultimately lead to the European Union was born.[3]

Considering this background, it might have struck listeners as strange that Chancellor Schröder chose the metaphor of the German way as a slogan in his 2002 election campaign. The first sentence of his speech in his hometown in Lower Saxony was: "Es ist wahr, wir haben uns auf den Weg gemacht, auf unseren deutschen Weg" (It is true, we have set off on our way, on our German way).[4] Critics accused Schröder of seeking to revive old themes tied to Germany's role in Europe and the world in the 19th century. For example, conservative historian Michael Stürmer ridiculed Schröder's "verbal claps of thunder," perceiving them as "Wilhelminian echoes." Others, like philosopher and pro-Europeanist Jürgen Habermas, considered Schröder's rhetoric a frightening turn away from the ideals of the Federal Republic.

Not everyone was displeased by the new self-confidence Schröder expressed. The "New Right" applauded him for finally leading Germany out of the past. According to a report in the weekly newspaper *Junge Freiheit* (Young Freedom), the Chancellor's rhetoric was not only "self-confident" and "courageous," but also exhibited the right instinct for how Germany should present itself to the United States. Instead of practicing satellite-like loyalty, Germany should from now on deal with America "auf gleicher Augenhöhe" (at eye level).[5] By presenting the country as finally grown up and capable of not only standing on its own feet, but also taking on a leadership role in the European Union – becoming a *primus inter pares* – Schröder apparently captured the *Zeitgeist* (spirit of the times) of the nation. Many found the notion of a European counterweight to the colossus United States under German leadership and guidance pleasing.[6]

Whether one interprets the Iraq war as a turning point in the transatlantic partnership or not, one thing is clear: the United States clearly did not expect the resounding "NO" of its German ally in the matter of the Iraq War. Even though the world's only superpower did not *need* German troops or money, a symbolic commitment from one of the driving forces in the European Union would have helped legitimize the war effort in the eyes of the world. And even if American leaders had not counted on any sort of support from Germany, they probably also had not expected the very outspoken criticism of Chancellor Schröder and his colleagues, election campaign or not. Up until 2003, America had always been able to rely on its "special friendship" with Germany.

Throughout the Cold War and during most of the 1990s, the transatlantic relationship had been a pillar of German foreign policy. Disagreeing with the United States was a *faux pas*, it was simply "not done." This remained true throughout most of the 1990s under the auspices of Helmut Kohl, Adenauer's "grandson" and steadfast friend to the United States. The devotion to the U.S. was at times so complete that critics referred to the relationship between the two nations as that of lord and vassal. Even when German leaders disagreed on a foreign policy action, such as during the 1991 Iraq war, they made sure to frame their disapproval in terms that would not harm the special friendship. In Kosovo, the German rhetoric focused – among other things – on the need to prove oneself a trustworthy ally to NATO and the United States. In Afghanistan, Bundestag members argued that the lessons of history demanded that Germany support the United States and thus repay the friendship received for decades, despite serious misgivings about the mission among a large portion of the Bundestag and of the German public. In Iraq, no such concerns about this friendship could be detected, at least in the rhetoric of the government coalition.

Although the political leaders of the United States at least initially sought to downplay the disagreement with Germany as much as possible, the U.S. Media apparently knew no such hesitation. Bill O'Reilly, host of one of the highest-rated shows on U.S. 24-hour news channels, asked German Ambassador Wolfgang Ischinger where the German refusal to support the United States in Iraq came from. O'Reilly said:

> We saved your butt after World War II. We rebuilt your country with my money, my father's money, my grandfather's money. And we protected you against the Russians in the Cold War, as you know. Now, Americans are saying to Germany, give us the benefit of the doubt, please. We believe Saddam Hussein is a threat to the whole world. ... Let us remove a person who is a threat to the entire world and you guys say: "Nein". What's up with that?[7]

O'Reilly's question, though perhaps not representative of the attitude of all of America, did raise the question of German gratitude and indebtedness, one that in the past had been raised repeatedly by German politicians themselves, most recently during the intervention in Afghanistan.

William Safire, writer for the *New York Times*, went even further in one of his editorials, declaring that "You can bet a German-owned publisher is going to get 'Mein Kampf Over Inspection' by Saddam Hussein."[8] This kind of talk – which would almost certainly have been considered an insult in Germany – indicated that no matter how diplomatically the American government may have dealt with the German "No," there were plenty of voices that were not afraid to call out the German decision, perhaps even considering it an act of betrayal in light of the history of the two countries.

What had happened between 2001 and 2003 that this time around Germany not only refused to aid the United States, even with a nominal financial or verbal contribution, but did so in a manner that was guaranteed to alienate the long-time ally? Was it election strategy? A spat between friends? Or is this case indicative of the future direction of German foreign policy? This was, after all, the first time Germany was faced with a choice between the United States and the European Union, and the choice was a meaningful one. As long as Germany's goals of furthering European integration and retaining a good working relationship with the United States did not contradict each other, the

German government was happy to pursue both.[9] When the two goals became incommensurable, Germany chose European integration, even at the expense of its relationship with the United States. What is more, it would do so again, should similar circumstances arise again in the future.

The main argument I put forth in this chapter is that the specific interpretation of German historical memory and the lack of national interests in Iraq – in contrast to other, European interests – led to the German refusal to participate in the U.S.-led war against Iraq. Though this case does not herald a complete break between Europe and the United States, it should nevertheless be seen as an indication of where Germany's foreign policy priorities lie, should a choice be forced upon it. It is also a sign of the continued maturation of German politics. A return to normalcy does not necessarily entail a return to militarism, but rather a return to a self-confident foreign policy that seeks to elevate Germany to a true leadership position within the European Union. The latter could – given the proper incentives, perhaps in the form of antagonistic American rhetoric and behavior – well decide to make the effort to balance the world's superpower.

Germany Remembers: War Is Bad!

Once again, historical memory and national interests both played a significant part in German foreign policy thought in the case of Iraq and therefore influenced the foreign policy rhetoric in the Bundestag. With regard to the former, there are no immediate historical memories about Iraq itself, but German memories about World War II, general beliefs about the use of force as a foreign policy tool, and about the notion of a German *Sonderweg* (special path) played an important role. With regard to national interests, the lack of such interests in Iraq, combined with other German priorities, contributed greatly to the German decision in this matter.

Perhaps the most noteworthy aspect of German memory in this case is the lack of any historically motivated (or historically justifiable) reason to intervene in Iraq. In Kosovo, there was a direct connection through the experiences of World War II in the Eastern European theater, which could be interpreted in such a way as to derive a moral mandate for intervention. In Afghanistan, the special friendship with the United States as a result of American aid after the war became part of the motivation. In Iraq, however, no such link exists. Granted, one might argue that the special friendship could once again be considered enough reason to support America's war effort, but the fact is that much of the legacy of World War II actually speaks *against* it.

Despite a certain maturation of German foreign policy thinking during the last fifteen years and despite a reinterpretation of historical memory in many ways, the legacy of World War II is not as malleable as it may seem. I argued in the Chapter 1 that some aspects of German historical memory might be more open to reinterpretation than others. The more internalized a certain memory or belief has become, the more difficult it is to reinterpret. German antimilitarism, for instance, had recently been reinterpreted to allow the use of military force under certain circumstances, though this certainly did not constitute a "blank check" for the use of force. Restrictions still apply: most importantly, multilateralism remains an integral component of German foreign policy thought,[10] as a result of the negative historical associations with unilateralism. Even in the cases of Kosovo and Afghanistan, Germany remained true to this principle.[11] In Iraq, the "coalition of the willing" could simply not be interpreted as satisfying the criteria of multilateral action.

In addition, Bush's rhetoric of the "axis of evil" and his black-and-white interpretations of the world scared many Germans who had grown up under a social and political system that – as a result of the Nazi legacy – instilled in them the belief that the world is perhaps best viewed in shades of gray and that the more fervently a belief is held, the more skeptical it should make one. A popular German magazine – *Der Spiegel* – illustrated in its edition from February 17, 2002, just how uncomfortable George Bush's rhetoric made Germans. The cover showed a picture of Bush holding a microphone while standing in front of a huge cross. The title read: "In Göttlicher Mission: Der Kreuzzug des George W. Bush" (On a Mission from God: The Crusade of George W. Bush). The edition contained several articles that criticized the simplistic rhetoric of the American government, which was interpreted as an attempt to legitimize its unilateral actions. It called Bush's religious undertones "fundamentalist sanctimoniousness"[12] and pointed out that "devout presidents can change the world for the worse by grandiosely failing in their attempts to make it better."[13] Perhaps more important than the Spiegel articles themselves was the decision of the editors to publish an article entitled "How Joseph Göbbels[14] propagated the 'total war' 60 years ago," right between articles entitled "International resistance to the war plans of the USA" and "Bush and America's warriors of God call for the final struggle," thus implying that perhaps U.S. war rhetoric is comparable to Nazi propaganda?

Bush's promotion of preemptive warfare also evoked very negative memories among the German elite and public. Any unprovoked military action would inevitably be associated with the Nazi wars of aggression, making it an absolutely inappropriate tool of foreign policy.[15] In a culture in which the use of force is still considered to be a last resort,[16] a preventive strike simply could not be justified.

The German National Interest in Iraq Is Peace!

The question of German national interests in Iraq should more appropriately be framed as a question of the lack of such interests. The German government had already refused to participate in a war against Iraq in 1991, probably for the very same reasons. In addition to a lack of direct German interests in Iraq, there were several factors that should disincline the government to participating in an intervention. Most importantly, the political and public debates surrounding the military intervention in Afghanistan had shown the Red-Green coalition that there was no overwhelming support for the U.S.-led war against terrorism. While in 1999 most Germans had supported the mission in Kosovo, the majority of the population expressed its disagreement with the mission in Afghanistan, both in public opinion polls and through participation in public protests. As illustrated in the previous chapter, Chancellor Schröder barely managed to get the Afghanistan resolution passed, having to tie the vote to a vote of confidence. He knew that he would not be able to easily sell the war against Iraq due to the fragile elite and public support.

In addition, the public discourse since September 11th had remained focused on the need to address the underlying social and economic sources of terrorism. A military strike against Saddam Hussein – whose connections to terrorist organizations had never been accepted in Germany in the first place – was simply not considered to be effective and therefore seen as a waste of resources.

The bottom line was that Germany had "other fish to fry." The wave of anti-Americanism was perhaps seen as a chance by Schröder's government to not only ensure its reelection, but to also push for further European integration and the advancement of a common European foreign and security policy. By framing the promotion of a stronger Europe as a necessity in order to be able to balance the unilateralist policies of the United States, German leaders hoped for greater acceptance of further integration among their own population and among their European neighbors. Werner Link, Professor Emeritus at the University of Cologne, suggested that the European willingness to reconsider its foreign policy baselines should be seen as a direct result of America's new national security strategy.[17] The U.S. desire to restructure the international system by way of "hegemonic, imperialist principles" produced the necessity for Germany and Europe to "determine their own political baselines in response to the American strategy."[18] German President Johannes Rau confirmed this in a speech he gave in May 2005, when he lamented that Europe had always had the potential to be a great power, but had lacked the willingness. He demanded that Europeans become capable of acting independently from the United States.[19]

The Political Debates: Government vs. Opposition

The Kosovo and Afghanistan debates had been remarkable, because both had revealed a great deal of consensus across party lines. In contrast to that, an analysis of the Iraq debates revealed a significant divide between the rhetoric of the government (SPD and Greens) and that of the opposition (CDU and FDP). In the following, the term "Red-Green" will refer to the rhetoric of the government, while the term "Black-Yellow" will refer to that of the opposition.

Despite their differences, the rhetoric of both Red-Green and that of Black-Yellow followed the same pattern (or rhetorical map) discovered in the debates accompanying the Kosovo and Afghanistan missions. Both sides claimed to abide by the lessons of history and to practice a responsible foreign policy, yet suggested very different interpretations of and solutions to the problem at hand. The members of the Red-Green coalition argued predominantly against German participation in the war against Iraq; the members of the Black-Yellow coalition, with a few exceptions, argued in favor not necessarily of the war itself, but of standing by the United States, even if that loyalty lead to war as the *Ultima Ratio* (last resort). This fact in itself suggests the malleability of the terms that have come to define German foreign policy. Figure 4.1 provides a map of the main themes of the Iraq debates.

Figure 4.1: Rhetorical Map of the Iraq Debates

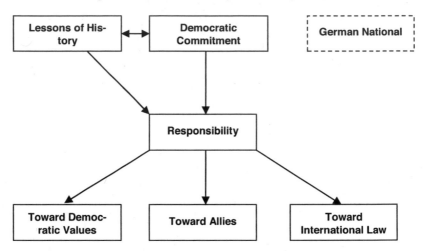

This rhetorical map is based on the analysis of three Bundestag debates, taking place between January and March of 2003. The relatively low number of individual debates compared to the first two cases is explained by the fact that the question of whether or not Germany would participate in the war against Iraq was simply not an issue. At least the government coalition had made it very clear right from the start – in fact, all throughout 2002 – that the United States could not count on its German ally in this matter. The actual debates therefore merely reinforced the lines already drawn in the sand. Nonetheless, the justifications of the decision and the divide between government and opposition make these debates fascinating.

The Lessons of History and German Responsibility

As in the Kosovo and Afghanistan debates before, German policy makers – irrespective of their political affiliation – continued to feel the need to justify their motivations with Germany's historical experiences in order to show that they had learned the lessons of history.

Chancellor Schröder, for instance, said in his opening speech that Germans "know from their own history that profound changes can only be achieved through long-term processes." Not only was he implying that it was important to be aware of one's history, but he also suggested that it offered the solution to the problem at hand. Joseph Fischer

(Greens) supported this notion by pointing out that "in light of our history, we make the decision of war and peace difficult, and at times extremely difficult. I do not consider this a disadvantage, but merely a consequence of our history. Nonetheless we are able to fulfill our responsibility." In fact, as became clear in other speeches by Fischer, he believed that it was part of Germany's responsibility to not take the decisions about war and peace lightly. That was the lesson of history!

On the side of the opposition, the rhetoric regarding the importance of the lessons of history – if not what exactly those lessons were – was very similar to that of the government coalition. Angela Merkel (CDU) proclaimed that German foreign policy responsibility was directly derived from history: "Especially we Germans, who ... have overcome two world wars in order to find freedom and self-determination, now have a duty to fulfill our new responsibility." Later on she asserted that "because of its historical experience and its geographic location, Germany has a very special responsibility in Europe." Her colleague Michael Glos (CDU) affirmed that "we know the lessons of our history," and appealed to his audience to act accordingly. He also suggested that the experience of World War II and the resulting postwar order "is the basis of German security policy." Dr. Wolfgang Gerhardt (FDP) prefaced his solutions to the situation in Iraq with the words that a nation "that claims to have learned the lessons of history" would act accordingly.

In the previous debates accompanying the Kosovo and Afghanistan decisions, all parties – with the expected exception of the PDS – had shown themselves surprisingly unified in the interpretation of the lessons of history. Dissent on issues had been minimal, and generally could be regarded as minor verbal jostles. In the case of Iraq, it was interesting to observe that even though both the government coalition and the opposition claimed to act on the basis of the lessons of history, the exact interpretation of those lessons differed significantly. In fact, each side accused the other of purposely misinterpreting history in order to garner support for policies that were really driven by ulterior motives.

For instance, Krista Sager (Greens) accused Dr. Angela Merkel (CDU) of '*Geschichtsklitterung*.' There is no exact English translation for the term, but it implies a biased view of history or even a "concocted history." The term also implies motivated agency, i.e. the person who engages in *Geschichtsklitterung* does so knowing fully well what s/he is doing. Sager told Merkel: "I had really hoped that today you would not try such *Geschichtsklitterung* again!" Her accusation was made even more consequential by the implication that this was not the first time that Dr. Merkel had engaged in such methods. In a country that is positively obsessed with its history and the lessons derived from it, such an accusation borders on insult.

Members of the opposition did not bridle their recriminations either. Guido Westerwelle (FDP) denied the claim of Chancellor Schröder that he acted in accordance with the lessons of history when he predicted that Schröder would go down in history as the chancellor who led Germany out of the community of states. He berated Schröder: "It is shabby that you, Mr. Chancellor, are not acting a little better and more history-conscious. Your policies are un-historical." Responding to Schröder's interpretation of the Iraq war, Westerwelle claimed that "history has shown something different."

While both sides asserted that they were acting in accordance with the lessons of history, the rhetoric of Red-Green focused on the memories of the terrible devastation and destruction World War II caused. It argued that those who truly knew the meaning of war had no desire to repeat it. "Never again war!" had once again become the slogan. Germany, because of its history, had a special responsibility for peace, a responsibility to avoid the horrors of war. A second lesson, according to Red-Green, was that unilateralism could never be the answer. The course of action undertaken by the United States with regard to Iraq was interpreted as a unilateral move, despite – or because of – the so-called "coalition of the willing." Finally, the lessons of the Cold War reinforced the lessons of World War II. Members of Red-Green declared that containment had worked for decades, suggesting that it was an adequate solution in this case as well.

The rhetoric of Black-Yellow drew very different lessons from World War II. According to this interpretation, the war had shown that dictators could not be contained or appeased, but rather that they had to be stopped; if necessary, with military force. Pacifism did not work, as the years preceding World War II showed. If the West had not shied away from using force against Hitler in 1938, the catastrophic consequences might have been prevented. Framed in those terms, the memory of the war not only allowed, but rather required a military intervention in Iraq.

Notwithstanding the different interpretations, the fact that the experience of World War II still loomed over policy makers' heads 60 years later confirms the continued importance of historical memory in German foreign policy thought and talk. Two interpretations for this unceasing preoccupation with the lessons of history are possible: either the policy-makers themselves truly believe that German foreign policy should be history-conscious in order to avoid repeating the same mistakes, or policy-makers do not really believe this, but are aware that both domestic[20] and foreign audiences expect a history-conscious foreign policy from Germany. Either way, history remains an important variable in German foreign policy rhetoric, if not in foreign policy cognition.

In addition to the lessons of history, Germany's democratic commitment was also cited as a source of responsibility by the speakers of the Bundestag. As pointed out in the two previous cases, Germany's democratic values are considered to be a result of its historical experiences, so in order to follow the lessons of history, one has to also follow and uphold democratic values. Not only that, but by virtue of being a democracy, of being on the "right" side, as Schröder had said before, Germany has gained a responsibility that goes beyond the mere lessons of history.

Chancellor Schröder said that "we will never leave any doubt that we make such decisions ... on the basis of firm principles. These principles are universal; they guide our actions as well as our alliances: they are the principles of freedom, peace, and justice." This sent a message to domestic and foreign audiences, suggesting that German foreign policy was safe and predictable, because it was firmly rooted in the democratic tradition. There should never be any doubt in the minds of observers that Germans would not repeat the mistakes of the past.

In a later speech Schröder added that "in its responsibility for peace and security, the federal government has always been guided by the following principles: we stand for the reign of law; we stand for peaceful foreign policy by way of crisis prevention and cooperative solutions; we stand for multilateralism ... and the monopoly of violence of the United Nations." Karin Göhring-Eckhardt (Greens) also reaffirmed that democratic values guided German foreign policy. She said that "we have to talk about our values, such as peace, democracy, and human rights, and we have to talk about how we will realize them." Similar to the rhetoric of Chancellor Schröder, this statement sought to communicate a sense of security to listeners.

The rhetoric of the opposition cited Germany's democratic commitment as a source of German responsibility as well. Michael Glos (CDU), for instance, said that "we are proud that we are an established democracy, that we are a respected member of the alliance ... that we feel responsible for the principles of the free world."

It is true that most democratic nations point out their democratic commitment as sources of foreign policy. The foreign policy rhetoric of George W. Bush concerning the war in Iraq, for instance, contains numerous references to America's democratic values as the basis for action. In fact, Bush frequently claimed that the removal of Saddam

Hussein was a duty derived directly from the dictates of democracy. What makes the German use of "democratic commitment" rhetoric different?

The close connection between German national identity, the lessons of history, and Germany's democratic commitment make it especially important for policy makers to continuously justify their decisions by referring to democratic values. The fact that Germany is such a relatively young democracy, and that it was forcibly made into one, has created a need to always portray/justify German foreign policy as democratic and responsible foreign policy. A democratic Germany is a Germany that has learned the lessons of history. And a Germany that has learned the lessons of history is a Germany that need not be feared. It has been the goal of German policy makers ever since Adenauer to regain the trust of the international community, to become an equal member, and to be able to pursue German interests without arousing the suspicion of neighbors and allies.

While a verbal commitment to democratic values remains an integral part of the foreign policy rhetoric of Germany, the exact meaning of this democratic commitment is increasingly open to interpretation. In the Iraq debates, there was a significant qualitative difference between the democratic commitment rhetoric of Red-Green and that of Black-Yellow. This is noteworthy, because it directly correlates with the suggested courses of action in the Iraq case by both coalitions.

The rhetoric of Red-Green was characterized much more by an emphasis on peace and dialogue, while the rhetoric of Black-Yellow showed a definite emphasis on Germany's reliability and trustworthiness as an ally. Both were closely related to the idea of democratic commitment, as Germans generally define it. However, the fact that both sides favored a different aspect of the democratic commitment in this particular debate illustrates their difference of opinion on what the right course of action should be. It also indicates the flexibility of the term, allowing for significantly different interpretations in the same case (Iraq), as well as between cases (Kosovo → Afghanistan → Iraq). Through their rhetoric, German politicians establish the meaning(s) of being a nation committed to democracy.

In addition, the rhetoric of Red-Green exhibited a greater use of what might be called "passive" verbs than the rhetoric of Black-Yellow. For example, members of Red-Green tended to talk more about *dialogue, negotiating, maintaining (peace), continuing* (policy), indicating a preference for the status quo. In contrast, members of Black-Yellow tended to use more "active" verbs, such as *fight, act, restore* (peace), *secure*, and *guarantee*. This phenomenon, as well as its implications for German foreign policy, will be examined in more detail below.

Germany's Responsibility in Iraq

Different interpretations notwithstanding, the main stated motivation for the German decision in the case of Iraq remained a sense of responsibility. As was the case in the Kosovo and Afghanistan debates before, German politicians on both sides rarely talked about German interests. Instead, foreign policy was almost exclusively justified as a result of German responsibility.

Chancellor Schrder (SPD) emphasized that "Germany has a responsibility in the fight against international terrorism, responsibility for the unconditional disarmament of Iraq." Even though his government coalition was against a war in Iraq, Schröder tried to clarify that it had not shirked its responsibilities in the larger war against terror. Schröder's mentioning of the simultaneous responsibility for disarmament and for peace also implied that a peaceful disarmament was possible. Perhaps to drive home the point that Germany took its responsibilities seriously despite the unwillingness to go to war, he added that "the Federal Republic – this needs to be made clear to the entire world – has taken on a degree of responsibility that would have been unimaginable a few years ago: responsibility in the Balkans and after the devastating terrorist attacks of September 11th." In other words, Germany was willing to step up to the plate, but not in Iraq.

Schröder's colleague Peter Struck (SPD) reinforced this message, bringing to the audience's attention that "Germany has proven itself to be a very reliable ally in the past years, through many conflicts and crises, as well as in the fight against terrorism." As evidence, he referred to the engagement in Afghanistan, where Germany "together with the Dutch has taken on even greater responsibilities at the beginning of this week." Perhaps it was due to the unveiled criticism of both the United States and, even more so, the German opposition that members of the government coalition felt the need to point out all of Germany's past successes as evidence of a responsible German foreign policy.

Krista Sager (Greens) spoke of a German "responsibility that transcends the current conflict, and rightly transcends it." According to her, responsibility had been and always would remain a pillar of German foreign policy. The situation in Iraq and the German decision were not only to be viewed in light of the current situation, but also with regard to the tone this decision would set for the future. Part of German responsibility was to consider the consequences of any decision; setting a precedent for preventive war was not part of the Red-Green definition of a responsible foreign policy.

The opposition, the CDU and the FDP, also made use of the theme of responsibility. Even though they did not agree on the course of action to be taken, they expressed their belief that German foreign policy was guided by a sense of responsibility. Michael Glos (CDU) reminded his audience that "in the 57 years since the unconditional surrender in World War II, Germany has developed into an equal, valued partner ... (that) belongs to the Western value community." As such, Germany "has a responsibility, now and beyond this day." German foreign policy had to continue to fulfill this responsibility, based on a "sense of trust that we must not violate." Dr. Angela Merkel (CDU) asked "What about our responsibility before our history?" Implied in this question was that Germany's past was the cause of German responsibility in the present. Merkel went on to say that this responsibility must not be taken lightly. It could not be that Germans fulfilled their responsibility selectively; "we also have to take on responsibility in the face of risks."

Germany's Responsibility to Uphold Democratic Values

Both the government's and the opposition's rhetoric asserted that their respective foreign policies were derived from Germany's history and democratic commitment, and that they pursued democratic values. However, they differed vastly on which democratic values deserved protection in this particular case, as well as on what the best manner of protecting them was. Figure 4.2 gives an overview of the rhetoric of Red-Green and that f Yellow-Black with regard to democratic values.
Members of both the SPD/Greens and of the CDU/FDP coalitions emphasized the importance of peace as a German foreign policy goal, although members of the former made much more frequent use of the term.

The rhetoric of Red-Green identified the *maintenance* of peace as the ultimate goal of German foreign policy in the current situation, which was why they refused to contemplate German participation in the war effort. The lessons of history had shown, according to this interpretation, that war was always bad and should be avoided at all costs. "Never again war!" was the message the government's rhetoric was sending. For example, Chancellor Schröder said that it must be the goal of the German government "to exhaust any and all possibilities for a peaceful solution to the conflict." He went on to say that "it cannot be wrong to make the most extraordinary effort for even the tiniest chance at peace." One of the slogans of his coalition indeed became "courage for peace," implying that in the current situation, war was the easy way out, while peace called for an effort, character, and courage. This kind of talk fit very well with Schröder's generally more assertive rhetoric that often contained subtle challenges to the postwar notion that an aggressive German foreign policy violated the lessons of history. By framing the German refusal to intervene in Iraq in terms of "courage," Schröder not only distanced himself from the policies of the United States, but also reasserted German confidence. Ironically, perhaps, an assertive Germany in this case was a Germany that refused to go to war.

**Figure 4.2: Responsibility toward Democratic Values:
The Rhetoric of Red-Green vs. Black-Yellow**

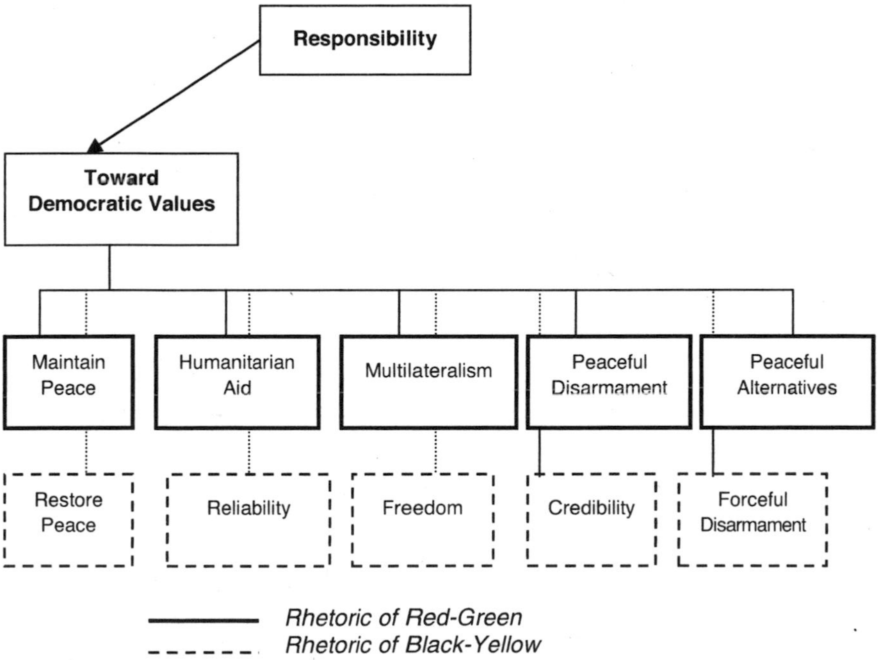

Franz Müntefering (SPD) also made a case for peace, arguing that it was Germany's responsibility to try to avoid war whenever possible "Where there is a chance to avoid war, suffering, and misery, it is necessary to take this chance to find a peaceful solution in the interests of humankind." The people of Germany, more than anyone else, knew the horrors of war "from their own experience." German responsibility to avoid war was directly derived from this first-hand knowledge of war.

Not only did the rhetoric of Red-Green assert that a peaceful solution to the conflict was possible and preferable, but it simultaneously denied that war could achieve the goals of those who promoted it. Claudia Roth (Greens) argued that this war would have "military victors," but it would not be a "political success." "It is not at all certain that [the war] will guarantee peace for the people in the region."

The special emphasis on a peaceful foreign policy was interesting, because it differed from the talk about democratic commitment in the previous two cases. In Kosovo, peace was the ultimate goal of German foreign policy, and its democratic commitment obligated Germany to do whatever was necessary – including the use of military force – in order to restore it. In Afghanistan, a similar rhetoric prevailed. In the Iraq case, peace was not only the goal, but also the method. In order to protect peace, one needed to act in a peaceful manner, as befit a democratic nation.

At least, this was the case according to the rhetoric of Red-Green. The opposition sang a different tune. According to Black-Yellow, Germany had a responsibility not to maintain peace – which Saddam Hussein has made impossible –, but rather to restore peace by ousting the Iraqi dictator and bringing democracy to the region. Whereas Schröder claimed that history had shown containment and deterrence to work, Michael Glos (CDU) argued that because of its history, Germany had a special responsibility to intervene in Iraq as "a people which is responsible for the Holocaust, because it was not able to stop a dictator in time."

Wolfgang Gerhardt (FDP) accused the members of the government of defining peace in the wrong manner. With their actions and their rhetoric Red-Green "showed a dictator that he could get away and continue his policies without having to fear punishment. [The government] has defined peace ... not [according to] the ethics of responsibility." What he was saying was that the desire of Red-Green for peace was noble, but did not take into account the reality of the nature of German responsibility. This idea was reinforced by Michael Glos (CDU) as well: "Pacifism may be an acceptable and honorable attitude of an individual, but it does not serve well for securing worldwide peace and for the containment of dictators." He added that "those who let Saddam Hussein be will sooner or later face the consequences of looking away." The notion of "looking away" had always been a sensitive issue in German political rhetoric. It referred to the period of Nazi rule in Germany, when most people had also been "looking away" and ignoring the painful reality instead of acting. Implied in Glos' statement was therefore that if Germany did not help to stop the Iraqi dictator, it would be tantamount to not having stopped Adolf Hitler.

The rhetoric of Yellow-Black, as it pertained to the value of peace, appeared much more active, if not aggressive, than that of Red-Green. Peace was talked about as something that needed to be worked for, that needed to be *guarded*, *secured*, *defended*, *restored*, and *guaranteed*, rather than something that resulted from passivity, that could be *maintained*, *continued*, or *subscribed to*. Peace had been lost due to Saddam Hussein's actions, and now had to be regained, whereas Red-Green claimed that peace existed, but would be lost due to the American war initiative.

With regard to other democratic values, the rhetoric of Red-Green made much more frequent use of terms such as *cooperation*, *multilateralism*, *humanitarian* (aid), (peaceful) *alternatives*, and *disarmament*. These terms were used almost exclusively by members of the government coalition, while they hardly figured at all in the speeches of CDU and FDP members.

This kind of talk by Red-Green was not at all surprising, as this had been a pillar of German foreign policy rhetoric since 1949. In fact, "not going it alone" had been one of the lessons of history. A German *Sonderweg* (special path) had to be avoided at all costs in order to not lose the trust and support of the German people and Germany's neighbors. It was the lack of sufficient cooperation by the international community that – among other things – prevented the government from lending its support to the war against Iraq.

According to Schröder, Germany was not abandoning the United States. It was also "not debating the existence or non-existence of NATO. We care about whether or not opinion creation remains multilateral." Not only did morality demand that international actions be supported by a significantly large coalition, but the matter at hand – that of the proliferation of WMDs – represented a "risk that can only be faced in a multilateral manner," according to Krista Sager (Greens). That was the "lesson the international community has to learn." In fact, "multilateralism is not at an end. The problems of the 21st century are so complex and intertwined that they can only be solved multilaterally."

The so-called coalition of the willing did not constitute enough of a majority to qualify their actions as "multilateral." The use of military force could only occur on the basis of very specific principles, which were contained in the Charter of the United Nation. Schröder said: "We know: even as a last resort of conflict resolution, the use of military force is strictly limited." As a result, members of the government coalition directed a good amount of criticism against the United States. Gernot Erler (SPD) found it ironic that the "war-waging countries now ask for the same patience in this war that they denied the United Nations and the majority of states." He claimed that "the politics of the American government ... from the start prepared the war and ultimately asserted itself against the majority of the community of states." It was "not Germany that [was] pursuing a *Sonderweg*," but rather the coalition of the willing.

The lack of this kind of talk in the rhetoric of Black-Yellow was somewhat surprising. Was this a departure from the old lessons of history, towards a new interpretation of what constituted a German *Sonderweg*? In the past, as well as in the current Red-Green talk, multilateralism had always been defined on a broad scale. Ideally, multilateral action would involve the support of the United Nations, and therefore a majority of the international community. On occasion, the definition became narrower, such as in the case of Kosovo, in which a lack of a UN resolution had not been considered an obstacle to military action, because NATO fully supported the intervention. In this case, the members of the CDU and FDP appeared to have lowered their standards for what could be considered multilateralism even more, implying that the coalition of the willing was enough to reconcile German participation with the lessons of history. Either the definition of the term multilateralism had changed, or the opinion of Black-Yellow about the necessity for German foreign policy to be multilateral policy had. The first possibility suggests an even greater power of political rhetoric. The second might imply a generational effect and perhaps a longer-lasting and more significant change in German foreign policy ideals.

Instead of ideas related to cooperation and multilateralism, the rhetoric of Black-Yellow emphasized a different set of democratic values: *reliability*, *trustworthiness*, and *freedom*. Those had also been pillars of German foreign policy rhetoric for decades. Dr. Angela Merkel (CDU) argued that "we of all people, who managed to overcome two World Wars with the help of our friends and allies ..., now have a duty to meet our responsibility." That was why it was "absolutely necessary, despite standing up for peace, to strengthen the future of these partnerships through a high degree of reliability of the Federal Republic of Germany." It remained somewhat unclear exactly which "friends and allies" Merkel referred to other than the United States, considering that neither the UN nor NATO supported the war in Iraq and several important members of the European Union actually opposed it. Nonetheless, Merkel accused Schröder and his government of "jeopardizing Germany's reliability." Germany's current foreign policy was "unreliable," and "we will have to pay for it dearly, because it jeopardizes the authority of the European Union, NATO, and the United Nations." Her colleague Wolfgang Schäuble (CDU) added that "determination, reliability, and partnership are the better way to guarantee peace for the future." In contrast, the Iraq policy of Red-Green "undermines Germany's reliability." Even if there was doubt about the situation in Iraq, according to Michael Glos (CDU), "it must be very clear that we stand at the side of our friends of the free world, our friends in the Security Council, and our American friends."

Those were the lessons of history! Wolfgang Gerhardt (FDP) reminded the Bundestag in his speech that "in the 57 years that have passed since the complete defeat in World War II, Germany has become an equal and valued partner again ... due to the trust that others have shown in us. We must not violate that trust!" He also warned that the foreign policy choices of Red-Green were leading Germany down a path that would isolate it not only from the United States, but from the rest of the world. "If one distances oneself from one's partners from the start ... and walks a *Sonderweg*, then one should not be surprised, if one stands alone in the end." In light of the events of World War II, which generally had been interpreted as being the result of an earlier German *Sonderweg*, this warning carried a meaning beyond merely the Iraq crisis.

Germany's Responsibility toward Its Allies

In the Kosovo case, support for NATO had supposedly been one of the driving forces behind Germany's decision to participate in the airstrikes against Serbia, despite the lack of a UN mandate. In the Afghanistan case, it had been the "special friendship" with the United States that had compelled German action. In both cases, the members of the European Union were relatively unified in their opinion, which means that Germany did not have to choose between allies. That changed in the case of Iraq! When Germany was forced to choose between the United States and the European Union, the majority of the Bundestag members chose Europe.

The Rhetoric of Red-Green
Considering how passionately the members of Red-Green had evoked the friendship with the United States only two years earlier, it was

somewhat surprising how unemotional, assertive, and at times even hostile their language had become when they spoke of the U.S. in the Afghanistan debates. What had happened to the "special" friendship?

According to Chancellor Schröder, this friendship had evolved into something more. "Germans and Americans have long been linked by more than just gratitude for the liberation from the Nazi regime and for the chance of a democratic reconstruction ... We are united by a friendship that is based on mutual respect ... and in which we can therefore have different opinions." In other words, friendship, yes, but on an equal basis!

His colleagues echoed Schröder's statement, albeit with differing degrees of hostility toward the United States. Gernot Erler (SPD) said that Germany needed to "lead this discussion with our American partners, but in the form of a friendship of open words and not in 'blind submission'." The notion of German submission to the will of the United States was not a new one. Over the years, the transatlantic relationship had been criticized by many as one that resembled a *Vasallentum*[21] (a lord-vassal relationship) rather than an equal partnership. Claudia Roth (Greens) pointed out that it had been the United States itself that had taught Germany to not settle for less than equality in its alliances. She said that Germany "owed" to America the "freedom of thought, the freedom of opinion, and the political argument even and especially with allied countries." That in this case the freedom of opinion should prompt the Bundestag to publicly oppose the United States did not change anything.

Most speakers of Red-Green remained very respectful of the United States, ensuring their audiences that despite the current disagreement, the German-American friendship was not affected in any way. However, some did not feel the need to hold back their much less amiable thoughts. Peter Struck (SPD) took offense to a speech given by American Secretary of Defense, Donald Rumsfeld, saying that he would "not accept that Secretary of Defense Donald Rumsfeld mentions Germany in the same breath as Cuba and Libya. This is unacceptable [and] unfair." For German Bundestag standards, such words were quite harsh. Christoph Zöpel even suggested that this might be the time to consider a more permanent loosening of ties with the United States. "It is not inappropriate at this point," he said, "to consider whether Europe does not partly have different interests than the United States."

Perhaps the case of Iraq was more than just a decision of war and peace. As Charles de Gaulle once said: A war brings to light things that otherwise would have remained hidden. One might consider the Iraq war a turning point for German foreign policy, having made apparent preferences that had remained hidden until now. Not only was this the first time that Germany had so openly and publicly defied the wishes of the United States, but the rhetoric of a large number of Bundestag members suggested that they might also be reevaluating their priorities with regard to their alliance in general. Even though there was no official talk about a break with America, the fact that several members even brought up this notion in a Bundestag debate, no matter how subtly, may illustrate that in the future, German support for U.S. policies should not be as automatically assumed as it had been in the past. This is even truer in cases in which the wishes of the United States go against the wishes of a majority of European countries.

In addition to calling for a more equal relationship with the United States, the rhetoric of Red-Green also contained twice as many references to France than that of Black-Yellow. It would almost appear as though the government coalition had chosen France over the United States.

Chancellor Schröder expressed his government's commitment to France by referring to the importance of the German-French relationship for the future of the European Union. "This parliament has always realized that this continent, this our Europe, can not play its role without the closest cooperation between France and Germany." He called this a "fundamental position" of German foreign policy and accuses the opposition of wanting to give it up for "tactical reasons." If that were to happen, "it would be terrible for Europe and terrible for Germany's interests within Europe." Other members of Red-Green echoed Schröder's feelings about France and the EU being the priority, even if that meant risking alienation from the United States. "Germany and France remain the motors of European integration," which was why "German policy can never be about giving up solidarity with France," according to Krista Sager (Greens). Secretary of State Rudolf Scharping accused the opposition of encouraging a foreign policy that would "lead to the isolation of France." Such a policy would not only be detrimental to the interests of Germany, but to those of Europe as well.

Both the United States and France had always been important allies of the Federal Republic, each in its own way. During the Cold War, the United States had been essential to Germany, because it provided protection and security. At the same time, the relationship with France was crucial for the creation of a truly functional European Union. Up until 2003, German decision makers had never openly had to choose between the two countries. When they finally did, the choice was made in favor of France and the European Union, at least on the part of the Red-Green coalition.

This was a major turn away from the policies of former Chancellor Helmut Kohl, as well as his successor, then Chancellor-candidate Angela Merkel of the CDU. Kohl had never made any secret of his desire to retain very close ties with the United States, even as he was pushing for further European integration. Although there had been some minor disagreements with American politics during his time in office, Kohl never would have openly stood against the United States or so harshly criticized its actions. Schröder had begun to change all that. The *Frankfurter Allgemeine Zeitung*, one of the major newspapers in Germany, referred to Schröder as the *Abrissunternehmer* (demolition entrepreneur) of Kohl's foreign policy. Others suggested that under Red-Green, Germany was witnessing a "re-orientation of German foreign policy"[22] toward a *Europe puissance* and a policy "at eye-level" with the United States. It was even said that the anti-imperial, pluralistic policies of France and Germany had become a hopeful alternative for countless other countries.[23]

Regardless of how serious the division between Red-Green and the United States was, the fact that the rhetoric of the SPD and the Greens called for a more integrated Europe, for a common foreign and security policy, as well as for a stronger European military may suggest that at the very least, Red-Green would prefer a more equal footing in dealing with the giant across the ocean.

Dr. Christoph Zöpel (SPD) said that "the geo-historical and geo-political situation of Europe and America is very different." That was why it was not inappropriate to consider going different ways with regard to one's foreign policy. For Zöpel, this meant that due to the proximity of Europe to Islamic countries a European policy should seek to not alienate them and perhaps cause a large migration of potential terrorists across insecure borders. He suggested that there were better ways to fight terrorism, and to deal with Saddam Hussein, than military force without a UN mandate.

Günter Gloser (SPD) argued that in light of the current situation, "there must be a common European foreign and security policy." This was necessary in order to "secure the future of our country, to further European integration, and to be able to meet the challenges of a globalized world peacefully together with Europe." What he, and many of his colleagues, were suggesting was that a stronger Europe would be better able to deal with the United States on a more equal basis, and to offer (peaceful) alternatives, should that be necessary. Europe could become a *Leitbild* (model) for other countries.

Krista Sager (Greens) said she hoped that "the world would learn from this disaster" that showed that "even the world's only superpower

... is not capable of establishing a new political order alone." For Europe, this should be a wake-up call. Indeed, she said, "the people of Europe more than ever want a strong Europe, especially in the context of their experiences with the Iraq war." She called this a great chance for the European Union, because finally people were thinking of Europe as "their" Europe. It was the disappointment with U.S. policies that increased Europeans' desire for the European Union to play a more important role internationally. Sager went on to criticize the opposition for making it seem as though for the sake of unity in the UN and the EU, Germany should agree to U.S. plans for Iraq. She said that "a Europe that has to say yes to highly dangerous policies for the sake of unity is not a strong Europe."

Although the European leaders had long talked about the need for a common foreign policy and for a common European military force, the fact that this debate was carried out with renewed interest in the context of the Iraq war suggests that it was partly dissatisfaction with the United States that brought the need for a stronger Europe back to the forefront of people's minds. The unilateral actions of the U.S., combined with the at times unfortunate rhetoric of American officials, served as a catalyst for the integration process. Especially in Germany, leaders had been forced to evaluate their priorities in a situation in which Germany's European allies demanded a different course of action than the United States. At least in the case of the government coalition, the answer was: *in dubio pro Europa.*

The Rhetoric of Black-Yellow

As became apparent earlier in this chapter, the rhetoric of Black-Yellow was very much concerned with Germany's responsibility toward its allies. Unlike the government coalition, however, the members of the CDU and the FDP did not appear to believe in choosing France and Europe over the United States. Instead, they argued that German policy should continue what it had been doing for decades: push for more European integration while simultaneously maintaining a close friendship with the United States. Most members of Black-Yellow were convinced that a choice between the two was not necessary, despite the differences of opinion regarding the Iraq situation. They harshly criticized what they considered to be anti-American sentiments on the part of the government coalition.

In contrast to the government, members of the CDU and FDP continued to speak of German gratitude to the United States as a basis for a responsibility to lend support, both moral and material. Michael Glos (CDU) reminded listeners that "without the heroic efforts of the

American military ... Germany would be a socialist Soviet republic today." His colleague Dr. Angela Merkel (CDU) also recalled a debt to America for helping Germany overcome two world wars and their consequences. As a result, Germany had a "responsibility ... that includes the participation in military operations for the restoration of stability and security." Wolfgang Schäuble openly attacked the Red-Green coalition by saying that "we owe it to American reliability that we have lived in peace for 50 years" more than we owe it to "the speeches of the Red-Green peace movement."

Going against the United States was not only morally wrong, but also jeopardized German interests in the future. Wolfgang Gerhardt contented that in a time of crisis, even if there may be some disagreement, "there can be no doubt that ... we will stand at the side of our American friends." The consensus was that Germany still needed America, even after the end of the Cold War, both for political and economic reasons. Michael Glos (CDU) asked about the consequences for Germany's economy, if "we remove ourselves further from America." He said he feared that German products would not be bought in the United States any longer, and that American investors would stay away from Germany. Considering that America was the "locomotive of the world economy," this would be very detrimental to German interests.

At the same time, the continued cooperation with America did not prevent further European integration, or even the development of a common foreign policy and a common military force. It had to be clear, however, that such measures should not be understood as "a counter-movement to American policy," said Peter Hintze (CDU), but rather as a complement to it. "European integration and the transatlantic partnership ... are the basic principles of German foreign policy," according to Wolfgang Schäuble (CDU). Those who "go against these principles – whether in word or deed – endanger the future interests of the reunified Germany." The fact that Schröder chose France over the United States was harmful in the extreme, as it "has always been our policy to not have to choose between Paris and Washington" (Schäuble, CDU).

Instead, a common European foreign policy was necessary, but one that "shows consideration for the transatlantic partnership. Challenges would only be met, if the United States and Europe were pulling on the same string again" (Michael Glos, CDU). The European Union had to "develop its own strength and self-confidence ... but we can not pretend that we do not need the community of values and interests with the United States anymore" (Peter Hintze, CDU). Simply put, "Europe and America have to stay together" (Guido Westerwelle, FDP).

With regard to France, the rhetoric of Black-Yellow was much more careful. None of the speakers openly criticized France for its refusal to participate in the war against Iraq. Instead of commenting on France's decision, the members of the CDU and FDP pointed out that the French had been much more diplomatic in their dealing with the United States, thus not burning any bridges, as Red-Green had supposedly done.

Dr. Angela Merkel (CDU), for instance, argued that "France is clever and experienced enough in diplomacy to not walk into this trap." Rather than categorically refusing any military participation, "President Chirac has always said: we will see at the very end how we will decide." In contrast – and here Merkel was implying that the policies of Schröder were much less clever and experienced – "Germany has arrived at a dead end and, unlike France or Russia, has no other outs." Michael Glos agreed with this assessment, saying that "it is a fact that our partner France ... always follows its own course initially, but in the end is on the side of the Western community." In contrast, Germany's clumsy diplomacy, or lack thereof, had committed Germans to a course of action that was as imprudent as it was detrimental to German interests.

It was interesting that many members of Black-Yellow also did not want to see German soldiers in Iraq. Many of them even subtly criticized the American decision to circumvent the United Nations. However, they all argued that Schröder should not have taken such an extreme stance so early on, because his absolute refusal not only alienated the United States, but also jeopardized the credibility of any Western ultimatums. In other words, the CDU and FDP would most likely not have agreed to a military participation in Iraq either, but saying so publicly right from the start removed any chance that Saddam Hussein could have been led to believe that the entire Western community was determined to use force, if necessary, should he not disarm voluntarily.

It is questionable how much of the rhetoric of Black-Yellow was the result of a significant difference of opinion, and how much was designed to make the government coalition look bad. In the end, the disagreement appeared to be mainly over the way Red-Green managed the situation, not over the basic question of whether or not Germany should participate in the war against Iraq. The only other disagreement concerned the future relationship with the United States. While Red-Green favored a more independent German (and European) foreign policy, Black-Yellow wanted to continue balancing the European with the transatlantic partnership.

Germany's Responsibility toward International Law

As in the Kosovo and Afghanistan debates before, both the government and coalition once again confirmed Germany's commitment to upholding international law. There are, however, noticeable differences in the interpretation of this responsibility from case to case, as well as within cases. In Kosovo, the NATO airstrikes, despite a lack of a UN mandate, were interpreted not as a violation of international law, but rather as "helping" the UN do its job. The argument was that punishing Milošević was in the spirit of the UN Charter; all that prevented a mandate was the inability of the members to reach an agreement. In Afghanistan, the military intervention was never really questionable from a legal perspective, as even the UN agreed that the United States had the right to defend itself against the terrorists. NATO's Article 5 served to further legitimize the mission in the eyes of the German elites and even the German public.

In the Iraq debates, there was – once again – a significant difference in the interpretation of the responsibility toward international law between the rhetoric of Red-Green and that of Black-Yellow. Figure 4.3 illustrates the main themes of both sides.

The Rhetoric of Red-Green:
America Was in Violation of International Law

Many members of the Red-Green coalition argued that the United States was in violation of international law, because it planned to initiate the war against Iraq without a UN mandate. Chancellor Schröder indirectly referred to America when he said that "those who want to use military force can only do so on the basis of the UN Charter." There were, he said, strict rules that govern the use of force, none of which applied to the current situation. There was no indication of an immediate attack that would require the United States to defend itself, nor did Saddam Hussein – evil as he may be – pose a severe threat to international peace. Schröder did not deny that Saddam Hussein was violating international law, but even though "Germany supported Resolution 1441," the resolution did "not contain automatism of violence." In order to go to war against Iraq, America needed a UN mandate.

Ludger Volmer (Greens) suspected ulterior motives on the part of the United States. "The goal of Resolution 1441 is the disarmament of Iraq," he said. "The goal of America is the removal of the dictator." The United States was therefore in violation of international law, not only because it had no authorization to use military force, but also because it was seeking to overthrow Hussein rather than merely forcing him to comply with the UN resolutions. Volmer also accused the American government of deliberately misleading the international community by claiming that there was a connection between the war against terrorism and Iraq. "Where is the connection between Iraq and international terrorism?" he asked.

**Figure 4.3: Responsibility toward International Law:
The Rhetoric of Red-Green vs. Black-Yellow**

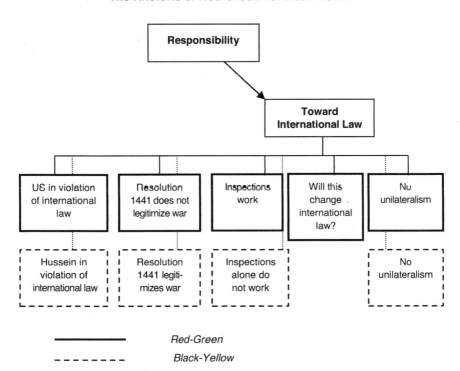

Gernot Erler (SPD) also worried that the United States (ab)used the September 11th attacks as justification for violating international law. He wanted to know "how it can be that the current rules of the world community are completely changed after the attack of September 11th?" According to him, "the most powerful country in the world has acted against international law" by unilaterally adopting a new security doctrine that enabled it to go to war against Iraq under the pretense of international security interests.

Uta Zapf (SPD) was concerned that this war was a preventive war. This kind of war went against international law, and Germany could "not support the legitimacy of preventive war." Zapf commented on what she believed was the U.S. government's plan to "use this war as an experiment for America's new anti-proliferation strategy on the basis of the use of force." Her party's politics opposed such methods, she added. In fact, European foreign policy was based on the preference of prevention over preemptive war, the latter being considered a violation of international law.

The Rhetoric of Red-Green:
Resolution 1441 Did Not Llegitimize War

A second important theme in the government's rhetoric focused on the interpretation of Resolution 1441. The United States had claimed that a new UN resolution was not necessary to authorize the war against Iraq, because all the elements for a forceful disarmament of the country were contained in Resolution 1441. Critics of the war argued that this was not the case. The same debate was echoed in the Bundestag. The members of Red-Green argued that Resolution 1441 did not authorize the use of force, but rather that a separate Security Council resolution was needed.

Chancellor Schröder pointed out that Germany fully accepted and supported Resolution 1441. "Germany carries this resolution," he said, "and has actively contributed to its implementation." However, he also asserted that the resolution "does not contain automatism of violence." In Schröder's opinion, the need for a new resolution was not an obstruction of international justice, as some might interpret it, but rather a guarantee that the use of military force remained a last resort. "No *Realpolitik* or security doctrine should lead us to incrementally accept war as a continuation of politics with other means." In German political rhetoric, *Realpolitik* had almost become synonymous with pre-Federal Republic politics; Schröder's statement therefore implied that participating in the war against Iraq would signify a return to pre-World War II German politics. To do so could not be reconciled with the lessons of history.

Schröder's interpretation of Resolution 1441 was supported by virtually all the members of Red-Green. Ludger Volmer (Greens), for instance, emphasized that Germany was committed "to the realization of Resolution 1441. We are talking about how we can force Saddam Hussein to disarm for good." That was absolutely not the question. However, since no part of the resolution authorized the use of military force, it was necessary to fully utilize all peaceful means available to the international community. If those failed, a new resolution could possibly pave the way for military action. Volmer suggested that the American decision to push for war might actually hurt the chances for disarming Iraq peacefully. He said that "if Saddam Hussein is lead to believe that he will be attacked regardless, the question is whether he would even have any incentive to disarm."

Gernot Erler (SPD) conceded that if weapons of mass destruction were found in Iraq, Resolution 1441 could be interpreted to contain the authorization of military force in such a case. Until then, however, the international community was obligated to pursue any and all peaceful alternatives. In fact, he considered it dangerous and irresponsible to strike prematurely. "Can we even allow," he asked, "that with regard to the core element of international law, the prohibition of the use of force, the burden of proof is reversed?" In answer to that question, Erler pointed out that "war is only admissible as a last resort."

The Rhetoric of Red-Green: Weapons Inspections Work
For decades, the use of war as a foreign policy tool had been unthinkable in Germany. After reunification, the German government reluctantly recognized that this position had become untenable considering the changed domestic and international environments. German leaders conceded that under certain circumstances the use of force may be inevitable. However, they always made it abundantly clear that in order to be able to even consider this option, all other options had to have been exhausted. The rhetoric of Red-Green continued to emphasize this belief in the Iraq debate. Before the use of force against Saddam Hussein could even be debated, it had to be proven beyond the shadow of a doubt that the weapons inspections had failed. According to the members of Red-Green, this was not the case.

Indeed, those "who want to abort the work of the weapons inspectors and replace it with a military intervention have the burden of proof," according to Gernot Erler (SPD). They would have to show that there existed an immediate and real threat to the world. If they could not prove this, the government coalition "refuses to repeal the laws of the international, civilized community."

Chancellor Schröder (SPD) made it clear that "the most important instrument for the removal of Iraqi armament programs is and remains an effective inspections and verifications regime. It has to be expanded and strengthened." No one doubted that Saddam Hussein was a dictator whom most people would like to be rid of. That desire alone did not justify abandoning weapons inspections in favor of military force against Iraq. Instead, "the weapons inspectors who work there have to be enabled to continue their work." After all, "the last mission of the inspectors in Baghdad has absolutely made progress." Because of that, it was Germany's "responsibility to enable the inspectors to successfully finish their task."

Gert Weisskirchen (SPD) reported that "as far as we know, (the inspectors) say that Iraq has begun to meet the demands ... of Resolution 1441." Even though there had not been enough progress yet, it had nonetheless been enough to insist on a "continuation of a prominent role of the inspectors." Weisskirchen reaffirmed Red-Green's commitment to "the full use of all instruments ... so that the alternative of war can be avoided."

Secretary of State Joschka Fischer (Greens) demanded "that Saddam Hussein fulfill his obligations, which he has not yet done, and that the pressure be upheld." However, the way to do this was not through military force. "The instrument for this must not be the termination of inspections, but rather ... the tightening of inspections." The time for the last resort had not yet come, because "the work of Blix, al-Baradei, and their teams offers a real alternative to war." Fischer also argued that between 1991 and 1998, the weapons inspections in Iraq had led to the removal of more weapons of mass destruction than during the entire Gulf War.

The Rhetoric of Red-Green: Setting a Dangerous Precedent
Another concern that shone through in the rhetoric of Red-Green was the fear that the decision of the United States to intervene in Iraq without the approval of the UN could constitute a precedent with devastating consequences. Or as Gernot Erler (SPD) put it: "This war is a bloody mistake which causes not yet recognizable political damage." According to him, the American unilateral doctrine "lifts the current international law off its hinges." If the decisions over which countries were allowed to have certain weapons, and which countries were going to be disarmed through the use of military force "are made not by the appropriate world organization but – if necessary all by itself – by the strongest and only superpower, (then) the Iraq war would become a precedent."

If that were to happen, the authority of the United Nations would be seriously undermined. After all, America's decision to circumvent the UN had taken away the monopoly of violence from the Security Council, contrary to the UN Charter. Krista Sager (Greens) summarized this very poignantly: "Saying yes to the Iraq policy of the U.S. government is saying no to the UN."

Heidemarie Wieczorek-Zeul (SPD) feared for the future of multilateralism, should the war against Iraq become a precedent. In pursuit of international order and justice, she said, "(t)he central role of the United Nations ... is an indispensable condition." Germany knows this better than any other country and therefore "cannot allow that the international agenda is changed." Franz Müntefering (SPD) echoed her concern, saying that "the lesson we should learn from these days and hours is that we need to find ways within the international community to resolve the question of who has the monopoly of violence." In order to have a chance to avoid war whenever possible, only the United Nations should be able to make decisions of war and peace.

Uta Zapf (SPD) worried that "the future of American foreign policy will be determined with this war against Iraq." Knowing that it was able to successfully circumvent the United Nations, America might continue to do so in the name of the war against terrorism. As representatives of a country that "has so long fought for the development of a multilateral international system ... such a tendency can not leave us cold." Such a development "would open the door to a new world order which rests not on contracts or consensus, but solely on the power to realize this order" (Gernot Erler, SPD). In such a world, we should expect to "witness a series of disarmament wars," such as the one in Iraq.

These statements seem hypocritical in light of the Kosovo debates only four years prior, when no such concerns for setting a precedent with the unauthorized NATO bombings of Serbia had been evident. In fact, circumventing the United Nations, which was seen as inefficient and in need of reform, had been interpreted as a favor to the organization back then.

The Rhetoric of Black-Yellow:
Saddam Hussein Violated International Law
With one exception – the need to avoid unilateralism – the differences between the rhetoric of the government coalition and the opposition were significant.

Perhaps most importantly, the rhetoric of Black-Yellow focused much more on the fact that Saddam Hussein had broken international law than the rhetoric of Red-Green had. Although the latter also emphasized Hussein's guilt and the need to force him to comply with international law, the notion of America's violation of the UN Charter weighed much more heavily in the government's rhetoric. The members of the CDU and FDP, on the other hand, pointed out that if Saddam Hussein had not been playing games with the UN weapons inspectors, the United States never would have been in the position it found itself in now. While not openly condoning U.S. actions, they placed most of the blame on Hussein.

Wolfgang Schäuble (CDU) cautioned the government against criticizing the wrong party in this conflict. He argued that if Red-Green continued to "direct each initiative against the Americans instead of Saddam Hussein, it will weaken the United Nations, weaken NATO, and destroy European unification." If the government wanted peace, it should "call on Saddam Hussein to subject himself to international law. If he does that, then peace will be secured." This message implied that the sole responsibility for this war rested on the shoulders of the Iraqi dictator. If he had not broken international law, no one would consider military action against him. Even now, he could prevent the war, if he complied with the rules.

Wolfgang Gerhardt (FDP) made a very similar point. He said that "the Iraqi dictator – let us be entirely clear about this – is the cause for the current situation. In the opinion of the Free Democrats, Saddam Hussein is the perpetrator, not the victim. He has failed to comply with 17 resolutions of the United Nations. He has violated international law many times."

Dr. Angela Merkel (CDU) also placed the blame for the war on Hussein. She considered it "a tragedy for the people concerned, who have had to suffer the inhumane reign and the wars of Saddam Hussein for many years, that they now have to endure yet another war because of this dictator." Her colleague Michael Glos (CDU) emphasized that someone like Hussein could not be battled with pacifist means, making the war a necessity. "Christians and non-Christians may be impressed by the Sermon on the Mount, but certainly not Saddam Hussein and dictators of his stamp. Those who let Saddam Hussein have his way will sooner or later accept the consequences of looking away."

The Rhetoric of Black-Yellow: Resolution 1441 Legitimized War
Unlike the members of the government coalition, most of the speakers of the opposition interpreted the prior UN resolutions – specifically Resolution 1441 – in such a way that they authorized the use of military force as a last resort. Dr. Angela Merkel (CDU), for instance, referred to what she believed to be a similar situation in the Iraq war of 1991. She said that "the attack of Kuwait by Iraq was answered with a resolution by the UN which ultimately was enforced with military means ... We must not exclude such military action as the last resort."

Merkel also made the argument that Resolution 1441 contained "the goal of peaceful disarmament through credible threats." In order for these threats to be efficient, the international community needed to show strong commitment and unity. According to Merkel, "unity in putting pressure on Iraq also includes accepting the consequences: military force as the last resort." Finally, she referred to the UN Charter, which "specifically contains the possibility to implement the UN's resolutions with military actions."

Michael Glos (CDU) also argued that if Saddam Hussein continued to refuse to comply with Resolution 1441, if he "continues this strategy, then – I fear – we have no choice but, as a last resort, use military force." Wolfgang Gerhardt (FDP) accused the German government of going back on its word by not participating in the war. He said that "the Federal government has agreed to Security Council Resolution 1441. This resolution includes all measures for the disarmament of Iraq, all of them."

The Rhetoric of Black-Yellow:
Weapons Inspections (Alone) Do Not Work
One of the main reasons why the members of Black-Yellow argued that military force should be considered was because they did not believe that weapons inspections alone would put enough pressure on Saddam Hussein to disarm. In fact, Hussein had fooled the inspectors for so long that he had not only compromised their credibility, but also the credibility of the United Nations.

Most importantly, without the threat of force, the weapons inspectors would not even have gained access to Iraq. According to members of the CDU and the FDP, the option of using force had to be available in order to lend credence to the work of the inspectors. A German government that ruled out military measures right from the start actually weakened the inspectors. Dr. Angela Merkel (CDU) actually quoted one of the weapons inspectors as having said that the German government with its policy of peace had made the war inevitable, though she did not specify which inspector had made this statement.

The notion of using the threat of military force in combination with weapons inspections was a major theme in the rhetoric of Black-Yellow. Dr. Wolfgang Gerhardt (FDP) claimed that with the threat of war, "the international community has tried to put pressure on the regime of Saddam Hussein so that he would allow the inspectors to return to the country." The policy of Red-Green had not aided the inspectors, but had hurt them. In fact, if the government coalition had had its way, "there would be no inspectors in Iraq at all."

In seems, then, that the opposition did not really disagree with the attempt to utilize weapons inspectors. Indeed, many of them initially expressed the hope that with the help of sufficient pressure, the inspectors would be able to force Saddam Hussein to disarm peacefully. They also emphasized that none of them wanted war. However, in order to avoid war, Saddam Hussein needed to believe that the threat of war was a credible one. The main point of contention was the way in which Schröder and his government managed the situation.

Both Red-Green and Black-Yellow
Disagree with U.S. Unilateralism

Despite their disagreements, both the government and the opposition disagreed with U.S. unilateralism in this matter. The position of the SPD and the Greens was already summarized earlier in this chapter: they argued that the United States, by circumventing the UN and acting unilaterally, had broken international law. Interestingly, the opposition also criticized the United States for this.

Guido Westerwelle (FDP), for instance, said that "those who want to disarm Hussein have to strengthen the United Nations. They can not weaken it by national unilateralism." Westerwelle emphasized that his party was committed to the "monopoly of violence of the UN," and that "both the governments in Berlin and in Washington have jeopardized the UN and made its job more difficult." He even spoke of a "pile of broken glass" that Germany and America had left behind in the UN.

His colleague Dr. Wolfgang Gerhardt (FDP) also criticized the American government. He pointed out that the friendship with America was not in question, but that "a military conflict without the passing of a resolution in the Security Council of the United Nations, and without exhausting further options of inspections, such as the American government has begun, can not be condoned by the FDP, despite the described circumstances."

Angela Merkel (CDU), who was probably the most passionate defender of the United States in this debate, nonetheless demanded that in the future, "we need a strengthening of the UN and a legitimization of its mechanisms, so that it will be prepared for new threats." She also reminded the Bundestag that there had never been any doubt about who should decide war and peace in the international system. "The UN should ... have the monopoly of violence," she said.

Is German Foreign Policy Schizophrenic?

Most notably, the Iraq debates represented a continuation of more assertive German foreign policy rhetoric, mainly in the form of interest-based talk. Policy makers across party lines had become more comfortable framing their decision in terms of national interests, as opposed to more idealist terms.

When speaking of interests, though, the members of the Bundestag appeared more concerned about European interests rather than strictly German national interests. In addition, they referred much more often to the European Union than they did to the United States as an important partner in German foreign policy. This represents a radical departure from the previous debates, when Europe certainly played an important role in the debates, but not at the expense of the transatlantic partnership. Most of the talk in the Iraq debates focused on the need for greater strength of the European Union vis-à-vis the United States and for further integration as a method for achieving it. That and the unusually harsh criticism directed against Germany's special friend across the Atlantic should indicate to observers that a significant shift in Germany's foreign policy priorities is occurring.

Gregor Schöllgen, a famous German scholar, wrote that during the winter of 2002/ 2003, "the points for a new German foreign policy were set."[24] He argued that the German government had distanced itself from the United States, and had indeed found a new self-confidence that would henceforth guide German politics. He was echoed by James Kitfield, national security and foreign affairs correspondent for *National Journal* magazine, who lamented that these were "the times that try the souls of transatlanticists."[25] The gap between Europe and the United States was deepening, he wrote, because the Europeans routinely bemoaned the Bush government's unilateralist tendencies and militarism which, coupled with an increase in religious fundamentalism, assaulted "continental sensitivities." To the Venetian Europeans,[26] who had long renounced unilateral military action as a thing of the past, America's new national security strategy would seem irreconcilable with their own foreign policy approach. Robert von Rimscha, Berlin Bureau Chief for the German daily *Der Tagesspiegel,* also examined the mounting German and European criticism of the Bush administration. He closely tied this turn away from the transatlantic partnership to increasingly successful European identity formation.[27] He argued that America is slowly becoming an "anti-model" for the future of German foreign policy, especially when it comes to the use of force and power.

These theoretical assessments were reinforced by the behavior of the European leaders themselves. In response to the European-American disagreement over Iraq, the Belgian Prime Minister Verhofstadt initiated a summit meeting of the leaders of Belgium, France, Germany, and Luxembourg on April 29th, 2003. On that occasion, the participants discussed concrete measures and steps toward a "European Security and Defense Union," which had originally been proposed by Germany during the summer of 1999, but had thus far not mustered the necessary willingness among the European political elite. That the talks were revived only five weeks after the beginning of the Iraq War implies that perhaps the American behavior and "you're with us or against us" rhetoric finally supplied the incentives needed. Even those who had routinely mocked the European Union were forced to admit that such steps were "historically unprecedented."[28]

That same year, Tony Blair, Jacques Chirac, and Gerhard Schröder met twice about the same matter. Their first meeting in the spring of 2003 had originally been kept secret, while the second meeting took place on September 20th in Berlin. In a subsequently published paper, it was revealed that the three had committed themselves to the further pursuit of a common European security policy, in particular the development of capabilities to carry out military operations without having to rely on NATO. The fact that this decision – as well as plans to establish military headquarters of the European Union – was severely criticized by the United States led some to conclude that it must have been an indicator that the decision was correct.[29]

This turn away from the traditional transatlantic partnership was a response to the way America was waging the war against terrorism, but it could also be interpreted as a result of a German Bundestag that was getting increasingly younger. Table 4.1 shows the age division of the 15th Bundestag.

In the 15th Bundestag (2002-2005), the number of representatives who were born after 1950 for the first time exceeded that of representatives born before 1950 (52.4% vs. 47.6%), confirming that the generational change might indeed be able to explain the change in German foreign policy rhetoric. After all, the younger generation of Bundestag members would not necessarily feel the same gratitude and special friendship toward the United States that the older generation led by Helmut Kohl had felt. They could also be expected to have less compunction about pursuing an interest-based foreign policy. At the same time, even the younger Bundestag exhibited a great deal of continuation in its decisions. Even though the transatlantic partnership might no longer be considered an absolute priority, a responsible German foreign policy within the European Union certainly continues to dominate political thought, even among those who were born during the 1950s, 1960s, and 1970s. In particular, the use of force should continue to be possible only with a justifiable cause, as an absolute last resort, and only within a multilateral framework, preferably a UN mandate.

Table 4.1: Age Divisions of the 15th German Bundestag (2002-2006)													
	Men						**Women**						
Birth Year	CDU	SPD	GR	FDP	w/o	total	CDU	SPD	GR	FDP	w/o	total	BT total
1931-1935	1	1	-	-	-	2	-	-	-	-	-	-	2
1936-1940	9	10	1	4	-	24	2	2	-	-	-	4	28
1941-1945	40	40	-	6	-	86	5	15	2	1	-	23	109
1946-1950	44	38	6	12	1	101	10	29	3	4	-	46	147
1951-1955	29	24	7	3	-	63	18	25	9	4	-	56	119
1956-1960	26	11	4	2	-	43	6	12	6	1	-	25	68
1961-1965	19	12	-	5	-	36	7	7	6	2	2	24	60
1966-1970	11	8	1	2	-	22	3	8	4	-	-	15	37
1971-1975	9	4	3	-	-	16	4	1	2	-	-	7	23
1976-1980	1	2	-	1	-	4	3	-	-	-	-	3	7
1981-1983	-	-	-	-	-	-	-	-	1	-	-	1	1
Total	189	150	22	35	1	397	58	99	33	12	2	204	601

Source: German Bundestag, 2006

BT = Bundestag
CDU = Christian Democratic Union
FDP = Free Democratic Party
GR = Greens
SPD = Social Democratic Party
w/o = No party affiliation

[1] The imperial adage was based on the believe that the German *"Wesen"* (essence) represented the untapped potential of an exalted ancient people, which could be used for the betterment of humankind. See Bernhard Giesen, ed., (1993). *Die Intellektuellen und die Nation.* Frankfurt a. M.: Suhrkamp, p. 74-75; Lutz Hoffmann (1994). *Das deutsche Volk und seine Feinde: die völkische Droge.* Cologne: PapyRossa Verlag; The nature of the German being was derived from German writers such as Johann Gottlieb Fichte (*Reason in History*, 1832), Johann Gottfried Herder, and Ernst Moritz Arndt (especially his infamous book *On People's Hatred and on the Use of a Foreign Language*, 1803).

[2] Jonathan P. G. Bach (1999). *Between Sovereignty and Integration: German Foreign Policy and National Identity after 1989.* New York, NY: St. Martin's Press, p. 17-18.

[3] See H. Grebing, ed., (1986). *Der 'deutsche Sonderweg' in Europa 1806-1945: Eine Kritik.* Stuttgart; Karl Dietrich Bracher, ed., (1982). *Deutscher Sonderweg: Mythos oder Realität?* Munich; Reinhard Kühnl (1987). "The German Sonderweg Reconsidered: Continuities and Discontinuities in Modern German History," in: *Rewriting the German Past*, edited by P. Monteath and R. Alter. Atlantic Highlands, NJ: Humanities Press.

[4] Speech delivered on August 8, 2002, in Hanover (http://www.spd.de).

[5] This was another of Schröder's expressions.

[6] See Arnulf Baring; Gregor Schöllgen (2004). "Die Zukunft der deutschen Außenpolitik liegt in Europa," *Aus Politik und Zeitgeschichte*, B11/2004, pp. 9-16; Ernst-Otto Czempiel (2002). *Weltpolitik im Umbruch: Die Pax Americana, der Terrorismus und die Zukunft der international Beziehungen.* Munich; Egon Bahr (2003). *Der deutsche Weg: Selbstverständlich und normal.* Munich.

[7] Bill O'Reilly Interview with German Ambassador Wolfgang Ischinger on Fox's "The Pulse." August 22, 2002. Transcript from http://www.germany.info/relaunch/politics/new/pol_bo_fox2002b.html.

[8] Safire, William (2002). "The German Problem," *New York Times*, September 19, 2002.

[9] As the land of the middle, Germany is no stranger to the notion of not putting all of her eggs in one basket. Immediately following WW II, the German government had hoped to pursue an active West- and Ostpolitik until the Stalin Note in 1951 forced Germans to choose. Even against the wish of the United States, Germany re-opened its Ostpolitik as soon as it could, during the 1970s under Chancellor Brandt. Because of its geopolitical location, Germany prefers to pursue a multi-faceted foreign policy, unless a choice is forced upon it.

[10] See Jeffrey Anderson (2002). "The New Germany in the New Europe," published by the *American Foreign Service Association* (http://www.afsa.org/fsj/sept01/Andersonsept01.cfm, downloaded on August 24, 2005).

[11] It may appear hypocritical that in Kosovo, Germans participated in the intervention despite the lack of a UN mandate, but apparently the German criteria of multilateral action were satisfied by the fact that the mission occurred within the framework of the NATO alliance.

[12] *Der Spiegel*, Nr. 8, February 17, 2002, p. 90.

[13] *ibid.*, p. 94.

[14] Hitler's right hand man, in charge of the Nazi propaganda

[15] George Seeßlen (1999). "Kriegsnovelle oder Wie eine Erzählgemeinschaft für einen moralischen Krieg erzeugt wird," in: Klaus Bittermann und Thomas Deichmann, eds., *Wie Dr. Joseph Fischer lernte, die Bombe zu lieben.* Berlin; Kirchen (2003). "Präventiver Krieg," *Frankfurter Allgemeine Zeitung*, February 6th, 2003, p. 2; Rudolf Burger (2001). "Die Politik der moralischen Militärintervention," in: Konrad Paul Liessmann, ed., *Der Vater aller Dinge: Nachdenken über den Krieg.* Wien, pp. 118-137.

[16] Ronald Asmus (1993). "The Future of German Strategic Thinking," in: Gary Geipel, ed., *Germany in a New Era.* Indianapolis, IN: The Hudson Institute; Clay Clemens (1993). "A Special Kind of Superpower? Germany and the Demilitarization of Post-Cold War International Security," in: *ibid.*.

[17] Werner Link (2004). "Grundlinien der außenpolitischen Orientierung Deutschlands," in: *Aus Politik und Zeitgeschichte*, B11/2004, pp. 3-8.

[18] *ibid.*, p. 3.

[19] Johannes Rau (2003). "Gemeinsam handeln: Deutschlands Verantwortung in der Welt," in: *Bulletin*, Nr. 41/1, May 19, 2005.

[20] Opinion polls indeed suggest that most Germans feel very strongly about having learned the lessons of history.

[21] See Thomas Risse (2004). "Kontinuität durch Wandel: Eine 'neue' deutsche Außenpolitik?," *Aus Politik und Zeitgeschichte*, B11/2004, p. 25.

[22] Werner Link (2004). "Grundlinien der außenpolitischen Orientierung Deutschlands," in: *Aus Politik und Zeitgeschichte.* B11/2004, pp. 3-9.

[23] *ibid.*

[24] Gregor Schöllgen (2004). "Die Zukunft der deutschen Außenpolitik liegt in Europa," in: *Aus Politik und Zeitgeschichte*, B11/2004, pp. 9-16.

[25] James Kitfield (2004). "Of Politics and Power: The Deepening Transatlantic Divide is More about Power Politics than Cultural Trends or a Perceived 'Values' Gap," *American Institute for Contemporary German Studies* (http://www.aicgs.org), downloaded on March 1, 2006.

[26] See Robert Kagan (2003). *Of Paradise and Power: America and Europe in the New World Order.* New York: Knopf.

[27] Robert von Rimscha (2004). "The Deepest Ocean after the German-American Clash over Iraq: Cultural and Generational Dimensions of the Transatlantic Rift," *American Institute for Contemporary German Studies* (http://www.aicgs.org), downloaded on March 1, 2006.

[28] Robert Kagan, *Of Paradise and Power*, p. 62.

[29] See Gregor Schöllgen (2004). "Die Zukunft der deutschen Außenpolitik liegt in Europa," p. 13.

5

Germany's Future in
Europe and Beyond

In this book I have set out to examine in what ways the Nazi past continues to shape German foreign policy behavior at the beginning of the 21st century, particularly the use of military force. I argued that a country's foreign policy is best understood as a complex relationship between foreign policy thought, talk, and action. German foreign policy thought is primarily influenced by two main variables: national identity (especially historical memory) and national interests, both of which are at least partly socially constructed. A constructivist approach can explain change over time, as opposed to more traditional political science theories which treat identities and interests as exogenous. An evolution of the interpretation of German historical memory – for instance as a result of a generational change – should correlate with a change in foreign policy behavior, as should a reinterpretation of national interests, perhaps as the result of changes in the external environment.

Despite the pronounced differences in each individual case and the different outcome in the last case, the rhetorical maps in all debates were largely identical. Indeed, they represented a continuity of the manner in which German politicians had traditionally talked about foreign policy since 1949.

In all three cases, the Bundestag debates followed this rhetorical map: The lessons of history and Germany's democratic commitment were frequently cited as the sources of a special German responsibility to practice a foreign policy that promotes democratic values, proves Germany's reliability and credibility as an ally, and promotes international law, as embodied in the institution of the United Nations and its Charter. While interest-based talk became more frequent from case to case, it remained a relatively minimal component of the foreign policy rhetoric. That is not to say that interests did not influence the decisions made, but rather that German decision makers continued to feel constrained in their ability to openly speak about these interests when they deliberated the use of military force.

German foreign policy rhetoric across the three cases exhibited certain characteristics of continuity rather than change. However, when systematically analyzing the individual debates in each case, it became clear that even though the cornerstones of German foreign policy rhetoric had not changed, the interpretation of the key concepts certainly had! The notion of responsibility may still have dominated German debates on the use of military force, but the interpretation of what exactly constituted a responsible course of action changed significantly from case to case. The same was true for most of the other key concepts. Table 5.1 illustrates the different interpretations of the lessons of history as a source of German responsibility examined in this book.

Table 5.1: The Lessons of History and German Responsibility

	LESSONS OF HISTORY	RESPONSIBILITY
KOSOVO	- Protection of human rights - Never again genocide! - No appeasement of dictators - Punish illegitimate use of force	TO INTERVENE in Kosovo in order to protect the Kosovar-Albanians and punish Milošević
AFGHANISTAN	- Gratitude toward the U.S. - Unconditional solidarity - 'Special friendship' - Reliability as an ally	TO INTERVENE in order to show solidarity with the United States and prove Germany's reliability as a NATO member
IRAQ	- War is not a foreign policy tool - Never again war! - Containment works - Weapons inspections work	NOT TO INTERVENE in order to maintain international peace

In the debates accompanying the decision to participate in the NATO airstrikes against the Serbs in Kosovo in 1999, the lessons of history were interpreted in such a way as to suggest that they not only allowed but mandated a military intervention. According to the rhetoric of the speakers in the Bundestag, the experience of World War II and the Holocaust had taught Germans that human rights had to be protected at all costs. Genocide simply could not be allowed to occur, and dictators who sought to engage in it had to be stopped – if necessary, by force. Appeasement did not work, as the Munich analogy illustrated.[2] Instead, dictators like Slobodan Milošević had to be removed from power and punished. The comparison between Milošević and Adolf Hitler in the Bundestag debates made this lesson even more compelling. The responsibility that derived from this particular interpretation of Germany's World War II experiences commanded the intervention in Kosovo in order to protect the Kosovar-Albanians.

Two years later, when Germany found itself called upon once again to provide military assistance, the lessons of history were interpreted slightly differently. The new interpretation was not incommensurable with the one employed in the Kosovo debates, but it clearly highlighted different aspects of German history. This time, the "lesson learned" was that Germany – as a reliable ally – had to repay the friendship received from the United States during and after World War II. America liberated Germany from the Nazis, relinquished its entitlement to reparations, and assisted Germans in the rebuilding of their country. Now it was time to return the favor by standing at America's side in "its darkest hour" following the terrorist attacks of September 11th. History demanded unconditional solidarity with the United States and therefore the deployment of German troops to Afghanistan. In addition, the fact that Article 5 of the NATO charter had been invoked made German military participation mandatory so as not to compromise Germany's reliability and credibility as an ally – yet another lesson of history. Interestingly, the main focus of the talk during the Kosovo debates, namely human rights, became all but insignificant during the Afghanistan debates. This should not necessarily be taken as hypocrisy on the part of the German policy makers, but it rather illustrates the discursive and socially constructed nature of the lessons of history that leaves them open to interpretation.

In the Iraq case, the lessons of history were reinterpreted yet again, this time in stark contrast to the lessons of the Kosovo debates four years earlier. According to the rhetoric of the government, history had taught Germans that war was never the answer and should not be employed as a foreign policy tool. Instead of "never again genocide" the slogan became "never again war."[3] As an alternative, containment was put forward. It was argued that dictators such as Saddam Hussein could very well be contained through a concerted effort the international community. Of course he could not be permitted to develop or own weapons of mass destruction, which was why UN weapons inspections were absolutely necessary. On the same token, inspections were said to work and therefore removed the need to go to war. The responsibility these lessons placed on German policy makers was to maintain international peace and therefore refuse participation the U.S.-led war against Iraq.

It may seem hypocritical for German politicians to radically reinterpret the lessons of history in the Iraq debates. However, due to the discursive nature of historical memory, more than one interpretation of what exactly World War II has taught Germans is possible. Even contradictory lessons are feasible, such as "never again war!" as opposed to "never again genocide!" Decision makers can draw upon different interpretations in different situations without being insincere. In fact, which interpretation is adopted is often only established through the debates themselves and depends on a number of factors. Firstly, the circumstances of the situation certainly play a role. For instance, the horrendous reports of human rights violations in Kosovo made the adoption of the lesson "never again genocide!" more likely than "never again war!" Secondly, whether or not there are perceived national interests matters as well. This is not to say that they completely determine which lessons of history are adopted, thus making the rhetoric "cheap talk," but rather that in situations in which the national interest requires a different course of action from the lessons of history, one of the two will have to give.[4] Arguably, it had been in Germany's national interest during the early 1990s to help stabilize the Balkan region, yet the lesson of antimilitarism was still strong enough then to prevent a German participation. In the case of Iraq, it might have been conceivable to adopt a different lesson that would have encouraged participation, but the lack of national interests made it more likely that this did not happen.

Just as the lessons of history and the responsibility derived from them varied across cases, so did the interpretations of democratic values, the allies Germans felt responsible for, and international law. Table 5.2 summarizes the findings.

In the Kosovo debates, the most important democratic values were the human rights of the Kosovar-Albanians, humanitarian aid, and the restoration of peace, which Milošević had violated. The main focus of Germany's responsibility toward allies was NATO, which depended on Germany's participation in order to ensure its capability to act and its credibility as an organization. Germany's responsibility toward international law expressed itself as the perceived charge to uphold the "spirit" of the UN Charter and punish Milošević, even though there was no UN mandate.

	DEMOCRATIC VALUES	ALLIES	INT'L LAW
Table 5.2: German Responsibility toward Democratic Values, Allies, and International Law			
KOSOVO	Human rights No genocide Peace (restore) Self-determination	NATO – institution NATO – members [German reliability at stake]	Uphold UN Charter NATO mission Punish crime Uphold int'l justice
AFGHANISTAN	Freedom Peace (restore) Democracy (≠ terror)	U.S. NATO [German reliability at stake]	UN Mandate NATO Art. 5 Self-defense
IRAQ	Government: Peaceful disar-mament Peace (maintain) Multilateralism Humanitarian aid Opposition: Disarmament	European Union Turkey Government: France Opposition: U.S.	UN monopoly No unilateralism Government: U.S. in violation Opposition: Iraq in violation

In the Afghanistan debates, the most frequently cited democratic value was freedom, i.e. the promotion of freedom around the world and the liberation of the Afghan population from the oppressive Taliban regime. Similarly to the Kosovo debates, the restoration of international peace was also a substantial part of the talk about democratic values. Germany's responsibility toward allies presented itself in the form of showing solidarity with the United States in the aftermath of the September 11th attacks. To a lesser degree, NATO was mentioned as well, especially after Article 5 had been invoked. International law was not discussed as frequently as it had been two years earlier, probably because the legitimacy of the intervention in Afghanistan was not really disputed.

Finally, the democratic value that was spoken of most frequently in the Iraq debates – at least by the government coalition – was peace, though this time it was the protection/maintenance of international peace, as opposed to the restoration of it with the help of military force. Germany supported the peaceful disarmament of Iraq through UN weapons inspections, and emphasized that the lack of multilateralism in the U.S.-led war was irreconcilable with the lessons of history. Perhaps not surprisingly, the majority of the speakers emphasized Germany's responsibility toward the European Union as opposed to the United States. France as Germany's ally in the European resistance against the war effort figured fairly prominently in the rhetoric of the government coalition. International law was interpreted quite differently by the two opposing sides: the government claimed that the United States had broken international law and that Germany should therefore not aid it, while the opposition claimed that it was Saddam Hussein who had violated international law, therefore making a German participation in the U.S.-led war possible (though not desirable).

Despite the different interpretations of the main themes – most significantly the lessons of history – in the three cases, it was interesting to observe that German policy makers had not adopted a new source of legitimacy in their foreign policy rhetoric. One might have expected such a change to take place as a result of the vastly transformed international environment following the end of the Cold War and German reunification. Indeed, the international community had made such a change fairly easy for Germans by demanding greater burden sharing and German activism. Instead, Germans continued to emphasize the importance of the lessons: a responsible foreign policy, commitment to democratic values, allies, and international law. The different interpretations of the specific meanings of the lessons across cases were the only concession to the pressures of the post-Cold War world. They allowed for a foreign policy that was suited for the changes in the external environment, but not so vastly different as to alarm the German people and their neighbors. The latter was especially important, because – as will be explained in more detail below – despite a generational change among the German population, the core meanings of the lessons of history remain intact. German politicians could therefore not adopt dramatically different foreign policies – provided that they even wished to do so – without risking the loss of public support.

For that same reason, not all lessons were equally open to interpretation. Some were more rigid than others. For instance, German reliability and multilateralism remained pillars of the Bundestag's foreign policy rhetoric. Granted, the exact definition of what constitutes multilateralism varied slightly, but there was a definite line that could not be crossed. This became evident in the case of Iraq, in which the "coalition of the willing" was not considered to be multilateral enough by both the government and the opposition to not clash with German beliefs. In addition, the Bush administration's political rhetoric about preemptive strikes against rogue states was perceived to be irreconcilable with German reasoning. Iraq in many ways proved to be the "last straw." Despite the lack of a UN mandate in Kosovo, at least all the members of NATO supported the decision and gave the mission enough legitimacy in the eyes of most Germans and Europeans. In Afghanistan, the issue of multilateralism did not come up, because international support existed in the form of a UN mandate as well as through the invocation of Article 5 of NATO's charter.

These findings suggest a path-dependent foreign policy, despite the different outcomes in the three cases examined here. They are also consistent with the theories outlined in the introduction concerning the need for incremental change in foreign policy thought, talk, and action.

German Historical Memory in the 21st Century

The discursive treatment of historical memory in Germany remains an important explanatory factor in German foreign policy. Shifts in the interpretation of the lessons of history – correlating with shifts in values and priorities – are at least as important in explaining German foreign policy behavior as national interests or even the mere institutional continuity, although the latter can at times be intricately linked to historical memory in Germany, as evidenced by the Bundeswehr and conscription or by the Basic Law.

Evidence that historical memory still plays a large role in Germany's public consciousness was presented in the introduction. However, I also argued that collective memory is by definition adaptable should the dominant discourse in a society change. The Bundestag debates in the cases of Kosovo, Afghanistan, and Iraq confirmed this as – 60 years after the end of World War II – the way German policy makers were treating the lessons of history had finally begun to change. No doubt a certain generational effect contributed to this revision in the dominant discourses of German historical memory. A comparison of the statistics on the age make-up of the Bundestag between 1998 and 2006 reveals a significant transition, as illustrated in Table 5.3.

Table 5.3: Age Divisions of the 13th, 14th, 15th, and 16th German Bundestag (1994-present)

	13th BT Total (1994-1998)	14th BT Total (1998-2002)	15th BT Total (2002-2005)	16th BT Total (2005-present)
before 1931	22	5	-	-
1931-1935	51	18	2	2
1936-1940	138	103	28	13
1941-1945	181	172	109	68
1946-1950	122	150	147	140
1951-1955	85	103	119	121
1956-1960	43	55	68	90
1961-1965	24	35	60	74
1966-1970	5	19	37	49
1971-1975	1	8	23	45
1976-1980	-	1	7	11
1981-1985	-	-	1	1

Source: German Bundestag, 2006
BT = Bundestag

Though no debates in the 16th Bundestag were examined here, the effect pointed out in previous chapters continues: 63.7% of the current parliament members were born after 1950, an all-time high. Helmut Kohl, himself born in the 1940s, once referred to his age category as having been blessed with the *"Gnade der späten Geburt"* (the grace of having been born late). What he meant was that he was too young at the end of World War II to carry any personal guilt. If that is the case for those born in the 1940s, one should probably expect any feelings of immediate guilt to recede even more for those born in the 1950s,[5] which in turn begs the question of whether their worldview also differs because of this.

At a first glance it would appear as though that is the case. After all, it was Gerhard Schröder and members of his relatively "young" government coalition who were almost from the start considered to be heralds of change. Schröder himself had pointed out on different occasions that his generation was not plagued by the same feelings of guilt as prior generations had been. And indeed, it was during Schröder's time in office that German troops were deployed for the first time in the Bundeswehr's history in a combat mission in Kosovo (although it should be remembered that the decision to participate in the airstrikes was made before the change in government), followed by the intervention in Afghanistan two years later.

It would be easy to explain this new assertiveness in German foreign policy with the above-mentioned generational effect. In fact, that is what many observers had predicted all along: as soon as Germans would "outgrow"[6] their guilt, the world would witness a German return to power politics and the use of military force as a foreign policy tool.[7] Unfortunately the case of Iraq mars the perfection of such a beautifully simple theory: the "youngest" Bundestag in the three cases examined here is also the one that most adamantly refused any participation in the war against Iraq, despite the negative consequences this decision had for the transatlantic relationship.[8] This suggests that there might be more to historical memory than mere age, and that the lessons of history are more firmly entrenched in the minds of even younger Germans than traditional foreign policy theories predicted.[9]

Nonetheless the nature of German historical memory is being transformed, though only incrementally. In addition to the more confident rhetoric in the Bundestag, this can be observed in public discourses across the country. The most important sign of this transition is the articulation of topics and opinions that were formerly considered to be taboo. For instance, it only quite recently became acceptable for Germans to publicly speak of the suffering of their own people during World War II. Before that, the dominant public and political discourse focused almost exclusively on Germany's guilt and shame.

The publication and – more importantly – the reception of two books in particular illustrate the new sensitivity toward the matter: Jörg

Friedrich's *Der Brand,*[10] a historical treatment of the bombing of German cities, and Günther Grass' *Im Krebgang,*[11] a novel dealing with the theme of the inescapability and negativity of the past. Both books climbed to the top of Germany's 2002 list of bestsellers, ahead of not one, but three Harry Potter novels.

Friedrich's book portrays the devastating bombing campaigns of the Allies against Nazi Germany which resulted in the deaths of more than 600,000 Germany, many of them women and children. The book's sympathetic point of view was received almost with relief by the German public: for the first time in 50 years, people felt as though they were allowed to openly grieve for their own losses.[12] In addition, the representation of the German people as passive victims who were caught between a rock and a hard place (the Nazi regime and the Allied attacks) – an about-face from Goldhagen's views of Germans as fanatical, pro-Nazi anti-Semites – fell on very sympathetic ears.

Grass' novel also represents a move away from the traditional depiction of the war experience. His book is an account of the sinking of the *Wilhelm Gustloff,* a big passenger liner, in January of 1945. The boat was filled with German refugees who were fleeing the front when a Red Army submarine sank it. Grass tells the story through the eyes of the narrator, an old journalist, in a way that challenges the long held taboo of German suffering. Grass himself said that "[N]o one wanted to hear the story ... [F]or decades the Gustloff and its awful fate were taboo, on a pan-German basis so to speak."[13]

The books, both of which would likely not have been published ten or twenty years earlier, and the public and intellectual debates that succeeded them, are indicators of a change in the way Germans are remembering the past. It is becoming increasingly acceptable to think of Germans as victims of World War II as opposed to vicious perpetrators of the Holocaust. Critics fear that this latest development in German public consciousness will bring about a revival of nationalist feelings,[14] as though it is only the guilt of World War II that keeps Germans in check. Following the end of the Cold War and German reunification, both Germans and Europeans feared "the forgetting of National Socialism, the doubling of German authoritarianism, and the return of a populist, excessive nationalism."[15] Even the above-mentioned Günther Grass expressed concern in 1993:

> The most dangerous thing is that we have [skinheads] in government. They are nicely dressed with beautiful hair. They speak well. But they think in the same way as the young kids who shave their heads and

carry swastikas and demonstrate. They encourage these ideas and these brutal actions.[16]

Table 5.4[17] further illustrates the transformation of German historical memory, but also suggests that an immediate return of German nationalism is not likely to occur.

Table 5.4: Public Opinion Regarding World War II (N = 1471)[18]	
Do you believe the expulsion of Germans from their homes at the end of World War II was unjust?	
Yes	77.1 % (1134)
No, the Germans started the war and are therefore responsible for the consequences	22.9 % (337)
The European neighbor-states accuse Germans of reinterpreting their role in World War II and increasingly considered themselves victims rather than perpetrators. Are you sympathetic to this criticism?	
Yes	36.0 % (525)
No	64.0 % (935)
How do you feel about erecting a memorial for German WW II refugees in Berlin?	
I am in favor of it	64.6 % (936)
I am against it	19.9 % (288)
I am indifferent	15.6 % (226)
When you hear that the Germans have to take seriously their responsibility for the Nazi period, World War II, and their consequences, what do you think? (More than one answer possible)	
There is not enough talk about the injustice done to Germans	55.8 % (822)
I am not very interested in the period between 1933 and 1945	1.7% (25)
We should bury the past	10.4 % (150)
I do not feel a historical responsibility for the Nazi period	36.9 % (535)
(continues on next page)	

In public, one has to consider each word carefully in order to not be suspected as a "Nazi"	48.6 % (704)
Because of our history, we Germans should use our influence to promote peace, freedom, and reconciliation in Europe	52.0 % (753)
The Germans have dealt with their immediate past very intensively and responsibly during the last decades	45.4 % (657)
Germany cannot ignore its historical guilt and has to meet its special political responsibility even today.	32.0 % (463)
A reticent foreign policy for Germany is still advisable	20.8 % (301)
None of these answers apply to me	1.3 % (19)

The answers illustrate the continued importance of the legacy of World War II for many Germans. For instance, 32 % of those asked said they thought that Germans cannot ignore their historical guilt and have special obligations even today because of it. 52 % said that Germany's history compels it to promote peace, freedom, and reconciliation in Europe. Only 1.7 % stated that the period between 1933 and 1945 does not interest them at all, showing that a very large majority continues to have at least some interest in Germany's World War II experience. At the same time, the answers confirm the arguments made above about the desire for remembering German suffering as well: more than 64 % of those asked responded that they are in favor of erecting a memorial for German WW II refugees in Berlin, and almost 56 % said that there was not enough talk about the injustice done to Germans.

Not everyone welcomes the softening of former taboos in German historical memory. Adam Krzeminski quotes Polish Piotr Machewicz as having complained that due to the reinterpretation of history that was taking place in Germany, people would soon start believing that "the Polish murdered Jews during World War II, and after the war, they brutally initiated the expulsion of Germans."[19] Lorenz Jäger even perceived a "shifting of the historical-political foundation of the Federal Republic."[20] Others thought they recognized the beginnings of a new *Stunde Null* (Zero Hour) that sought to put the final stroke on the legacy of World War II.[21]

The heated debates accompanying the release of the German film *Der Untergang* (Downfall) about the final days in the life of Adolf Hitler further elucidate the clash between those who are *geschichts-*

versessen (obsessed with history) and those who are *geschichts-vergessen* (forgetting of history), i.e. those who endorse the continued importance of the World War II legacy and collective guilt and those who argue that it is time to move on.[22] The film itself was highly controversial because of its humanization of Hitler – thus far a complete taboo in Germany. It was also criticized for glorifying the past by focusing almost exclusively on German civilians and children as victims of the war. Jan-Oliver Decker, a German historian, said in an interview with a German TV station that the film was nothing more than a "ghost train designed to overcome collective trauma." He denunciated it for leaving too many questions open, for instance the questions of why people were so fascinated by Hitler, why they were seduced. If one wants to learn the lessons of history, these are important things to know. Decker also criticized the film for not paying enough attention to the Holocaust. "I wonder," he asked, "whether one should be allowed to make a film about National Socialism in which the only reference to the Holocaust of 6 million people is a plaque at the end of the movie."[23]

All the examples illustrated above – the increasingly assertive rhetoric of the Bundestag, the remembrance of German victims during the war, the refusal of younger generations to feel guilty for the Holocaust, and the humanization of Adolf Hitler – point to a definite shift in historical memory, most likely as the result of generational change. Nonetheless, the extent of this shift should not be overestimated. It does not warrant fears of a returning aggressive nationalism.

Despite the changes in Germany's historical memory that have somewhat reduced the importance of collective guilt as part of national identity, there are certain areas of German public life in which the continued legacy of World War II can still be observed. A case in point is the refusal to abolish conscription.[24] The practice was introduced on July 21st, 1956, with the conscription law, obligating all male citizens of Germany over the age of 18 to serve in the military. The purpose was to ensure that the military would always be anchored in German society, rather than risking the abuse of a professional military by corrupt leaders. The Bundeswehr was specifically designed to be a *Volksarmee* (an army of the people), made up of *Staatsbürger in Uniform* (citizens in uniform).

After the end of the Cold war, critics began to question the practicability and necessity of the conscription practice. They claimed that it was outdated and inefficient,[25] especially considering the increasingly shorter times of mandatory service (from 18 months in 1960 to only 9 months in 2003). In most other European countries the trend has been to move away from mandatory military service in favor of smaller, more specialized, and better trained, professional forces.

Nonetheless, conscription endures in 21ˢᵗ century Germany. On the occasion of the 50ᵗʰ anniversary of the Bundeswehr, Gerhard Schröder reaffirmed his party's belief in the practice, saying that the Bundeswehr had been a "belated child of the Federal Republic, but was from the first day an army of the people and an army of democracy."[26] He also referred to the extraordinarily high level of acceptance among the general population of both the Bundeswehr and conscription. He claimed that this was due to the fact that the Bundeswehr "did not continue the detrimental tradition of the early German militarism."[27] Even hard-core realist Geoffrey van Orden admitted that the "debate over conscription goes to the heart of the contemporary German dilemma over the function of the armed forces."[28]

Even sixty years after the end of World War II, mandatory military service for German men is considered to be an insurance against a right-wing takeover of the Bundeswehr. This suggests that Germans are still very sensitive to the original reasons for firmly anchoring the military in German society.

Steve Crawshaw points to yet another continuing taboo as an attestation of the significance of the World War II legacy in contemporary Germany. In an article published by *Der Spiegel* he wrote that Hitler's book *Mein Kampf* "can be found in good bookshops in London, Paris and New York."[29] Yet in Germany this would be unthinkable, even though the cover blurb of the book notes that it is "necessary reading material for those who seek to understand the Holocaust ... and for those who care to safeguard democracy." Crawshaw argued that this was a sign that Germans had not yet dealt with their past.

Finally, the ceaseless historical debates that have accompanied the move of the German Bundestag from Bonn back to Berlin indicate that the past has not yet passed in Germany's collective consciousness. Though the move, along with the complete reconstruction of many of the official governmental buildings, had initially been hailed as a "reinvention" of Germany, it soon became clear that it was anything but. For example, the reconstruction of the old into the new Reichstag building was supposed to represent a break with the past. Yet when the architect in charge of the design wanted grey benches for the representatives, the government decided that the color grey was too fascist. Instead, the color blue was adopted as a more "democratic color."

Around the same time a highly publicized debate over the shape of the German eagle in the debating chamber of the Bundestag took place. Critics had lamented that the old eagle used during the time of the Federal Republic resembled a "fat chicken" and was therefore not an appropriate symbol of the reunified Germany. At the same time, initial designs by artist Norman Foster were considered to be too evocative of the hostile-looking prewar version of the national bird. A compromise was struck in the end, but the fact that Germans remain fearful of sending the wrong signals with their architecture and national symbols illustrates that historical memory is very much alive in 21st century Germany.

The Historical Memory of East Germans

It should be noted that the discussion of historical memory thus far has focused exclusively on West German interpretations of the past. It stands to reason that the way World War II was remembered under the communist regime in Eastern Germany differed substantially from these interpretations. Indeed, the East German remembrance tended to focus much more on the victimization of East Germans at the hands of the Nazis, followed by West German capitalists.[30] Historian Jürgen Kocka argued that the National Socialist regime played "a less central, less formative role" for East Germans than for West Germans, who see in the Nazi regime a negative reference system against which "they measure and judge their own society."[31] As a result, East Germans did not consider the legacy of the Third Reich part of their own history immediately after German reunification. Interestingly, however, a study carried out by Harald Welzer and colleagues on the basis of a survey about history consciousness among workers in East and West Germany in the mid-1990s revealed that even though East Germans do not share the Western historical memory, their own postwar memory has produced similar notions of collective guilt and shame for having tolerated the activities of the Stasi under the oppressive communist regime.[32]

Unfortunately there were too few Bundestag members from East Germany who actually got to speak in front of the Bundestag during any of the debates examined in this book to allow for a meaningful comparison of the rhetoric of East and West German representatives, unless one considers the PDS, the successor party to the East German SED (*Sozialistische Einheitspartei Deutschlands*) representative of more general East German sentiments. This seems problematic due to the fact that the PDS held only 30 out of 672 seats in the 13th Bundestag, and 36 out of 669 seats in the 14th Bundestag. The party failed to reach the 5 % hurdle necessary for representation in the 15th Bundestag.

Empirical data from other sources suggests that even though East Germans may not share the same guilt for World War II, the memory of the war is still very much alive. East Germans tend to be even more opposed to the use of force in foreign policy than West Germans, according to opinion polls. Most likely, the Soviet system was just as efficient at "re-educating" East Germans as the Western Allies were, though perhaps by means of different historical narratives.

How German National Identity is Changing

A good German is a good European
– Former Chancellor Helmut Kohl

I argued earlier that with the change in German historical memory due to a generational effect we might expect a return of the "German Question." Even though none of Germany's neighbors probably expect it to start World War III, a certain ambivalence about Germans and their politics is undeniable. Harvard historian Steven Ozment stated that because the tragedies of the 1930s and 1940s are becoming "less German" with every new generation of Germans, there may soon arise "rumblings of an old German culture preparing to return to the warrior days of blood and iron."[33] In fact, some European observers interpreted Chancellor Schröder's push for European reforms "as further proof of Germany's primordial drive to project power beyond its national borders."[34] Even if these fears are unfounded, "the consistency with which the notion of a 'German Question' returns to both the scholarly and diplomatic agenda should serve as sufficient evidence that Germany is not (yet) considered a 'normal' country."[35]

Perhaps such concerns are understandable considering not only Germany's past, but also its geographic location at the center of Europe. As the land of the middle, Germany is predestined to always be a serious player in European politics for at least two reasons: firstly, Germany will always have an incentive to ensure a powerful position for itself, and secondly, the rest of Europe will always have an incentive to let it.

Regarding the first claim, the fact that Germany shares borders with nine other countries dictates a foreign policy that minimizes the potential threat that comes with such a vulnerable position. In the past, Germany had tried to secure itself by way of an aggressive nationalism, seeking to establish its European hegemony on more than one occasion.[36] Nowadays, Germany is no less concerned with securing itself, but has found that – partly out of necessity – a "soft power" approach suits its purposes much better. Since the end of World War II, German politicians have perfected the use of their diplomatic and economic influence and as a result, have come to lead the very institutions designed to contain Germany after the war. Today, Germany is not only one of the main powers in the European Union, but it trades and invests more in Central and Eastern Europe than all the other Western European countries combined, therefore making it a potentially ideal candidate for regional hegemony once again, albeit a more benevolent hegemony than before.

A second reason why Germany should always be considered a serious player is because even though Europeans might feel uneasy about a strong Germany, they also cannot afford for Germany to be weak. Every time this dilemma surfaced after the war, the decision between a strong and a weak Germany was frequently made in favor of the former, despite occasionally serious misgivings. For instance, the Morgenthau Plan, whose primary goal would have been "converting Germany into a country primarily agricultural and pastoral in its character,"[37] was abandoned in 1946 in favor of the Marshall Plan. One of the main reasons was the realization that "[a]n orderly, prosperous Europe requires the economic contributions of a stable and productive Germany."[38] When West Germany was allowed to rearm and join NATO in 1955, many – especially the French – displayed qualms over that decision. Indeed, a British band played the German national anthem on that day because a French band refused to play it. Nonetheless, the fourteen European ministers who gave brief speeches on that day all expressed their belief that Germany's inclusion would strengthen Europe. Finally, the negotiations of the "Treaty on the Final Settlement with Regard to Germany" (or the Two-Plus-Four Treaty) in 1990 was surrounded by debates of the German question, i.e. German trustworthiness. Both Mikhail Gorbachev and Margaret Thatcher had serious concerns and expressed them quite freely. They feared that a unified Germany would be too big for Europe to contain and might once again pose a threat to European stability. In the end, it was decided that the unification of Germany constituted a "significant contribution to peace and stability in Europe."[39] All these decisions confirm the fact that a weak Germany is likely to produce a weak Europe.

Nonetheless, the unease that surrounded all of these decisions remains even sixty years after the end of the war. The assertive foreign policy rhetoric of Chancellor Schröder, especially following the rift in the transatlantic partnership, has done little to alleviate such fears. His declaration that "German foreign policy is made in Berlin, not in Washington" was only one of many expressions of Germany's new-found confidence. Former Secretary of Defense Peter Struck's announcement that he wants to prepare the German military for "operations around the globe" added to the heightened suspicions about Germany's future aspirations. Around the same time, the Spanish newspaper *Corriere della Serra* ran an article on the American-European crisis which read that "in the darkness of the crisis, Germany remembers that it is Germany. Berlin once again becomes the location where every European initiative is begun."

The potential for a return to power is undeniably present in Germany. Whether the willingness is there as well remains to be seen. Many have argued that the future of German foreign policy will largely depend on the evolution of German national identity in connection with the evolution of historical memory,[40] though there is a lack of consensus among observers about the direction that Germany identity is likely to take in the 21st century.

There are some demands to bury the negative nationalism Germans have held for so long and replace it with a "defensive nationalism" that allows for pride of territorial, ethnic, and cultural strengths, but not at the expense of other nations.[41] Others warn of the dangers associated with a traditional national identity (as opposed to *Verfassungspatri-otismus*, i.e. constitutional patriotism)[42] and claim Germany needs a form of national identification without the dangers of nationalist polarization and exclusion of other nations. Maybe this identification will come in the form of a post-national identity on the basis of universal human rights ideals.[43] Proponents of this argue that it will follow from EU enlargement and from the expected increase in migration among the European member states.

Judging from public opinion data, there has not been any sign of a resurgence of exaggerated nationalist feelings among the German population. On the contrary! Many Germans – in East and West – remain very skeptical and cautious in their attitudes toward nationalism and patriotism, as illustrated in table 5.5.

One of the favorite slogans among German citizens is that nationalism is "pure chance" (19.2% of West Germans, 18.0% of East Germans, but only 9% of average Europeans). Very few Germans believe that nationalism is a citizen's duty (9.5% West, 9.2% East, but a total of 23.6% of Europeans), but quite a few feel that nationalism is potentially dangerous (13.8% West, 11.8% East, yet only 7.7% of other Europeans) and arrogant (7.5% West, 9.5% East, only 2.6% of other Europeans).

Table 5.5: Opinions About National Pride 1994

	West Germans	East Germans	European Average w/o Germans
Duty	9.5 %	9.7 %	23.6 %
Natural	40.0 %	44.9 %	50.3 %
Coincidence/ Nonsense	19.2 %	18.0 %	9.0 %
Individual/ Nonsense	10.0 %	6.1 %	6.9 %
Arrogant	7.5 %	9.5 %	2.6 %
Dangerous	13.8 %	11.8 %	7.7 %

Survey Question: On this list you will find several opinions about national pride. Please indicate which opinions you personally agree with the most. A – National pride is a good citizen's duty; B – National pride is natural and goes without saying; C – National pride is nonsense, because a person's nationality is coincidence; D – National pride is nonsense, because each individual is different; E – National pride is arrogant, because it is directed against people of other nationalities; F – National pride is dangerous, because it leads to extreme nationalism and even war; (G – None of the above; coded as missing variable)
Source: Eurobarometer Nr. 42

Extreme nationalism in Germany is a peripheral phenomenon. There was a very brief surge of nationalistically motivated hate crimes against foreigners immediately following reunification, but overall Germans' national pride actually decreased in the years following unification,[44] probably as a result of financial burdens, internal tensions, and shame over the hate crimes against Turkish guest workers in Solingen in 1993. Whatever the reason, Germany remains far below the European average, despite an increasing belief that national pride is something natural. In addition, it should be noted that certain receding trends in Germans' identification with Europe are not correlated with rising numbers in their identification with Germany.

Nonetheless change has occurred in Germans' national pride, namely in the things they feel proud about.[45] Up until the 1960s, Germans had mostly been proud of areas far removed from politics, especially economics. This should not be surprising given the temporal proximity to the events of World War II and the occurrence of the economic miracle. By the late 1970s, citizens had become quite proud of the political system of the Federal Republic of Germany, particularly the Basic Law and the welfare state as symbols thereof.[46] Culture, research, and sports have been of medium importance as a source of pride, while the Bundestag has remained largely unimportant. In East Germany, national pride was more focused on economics and less on democracy, although that is now changing.

The overall lack of national pride in both East and West Germany can mainly be attributed to the legacy of World War II – both versions. Unlike other Europeans, Germans do not believe in an unconditional, and therefore uncritical, national pride. One might even say that their historical experience has caused Germans to deny the desirability of national pride as the result of a "damaged" national identity.[47]

Even though a return to aggressive nationalism as the basis for German national identity should be ruled out, changes do lie ahead. Most importantly, Germany has yet to develop an identity that accommodates its new position of power in the international system. The discourses on the use of military force examined in this book are the expression of the search for an identity somewhere between a civilian power and a military power, one that can be reconciled with the practical demands of the 21st century, but that has none of the negative connotations of previous incarnations of German militarism. The missions in Kosovo, Afghanistan, and Iraq have provided the context for "testing" interpretations of identity. Apparently, the primary fault line was Iraq and the lack of multilateralism in the war. Germany's new national identity remains very similar to the old one: a hesitant attitude toward the use of force, a continued commitment to multilateralism and German reliability, but also a new sense of responsibility that allows the use of force as a last resort, as long as one does not engage in "adventures," as Gerhard Schröder put it.

German national identity will probably also lose its extreme focus on the transatlantic partnership, as this was the result of deep feelings of gratitude and commitment shared by Kohl's generation, but perhaps not by younger Germans. This is reinforced by the disagreements between the "old Europe" and the United States surrounding the 2003 Iraq War.[48] Schröder's generation has become less reverent and less awed by the transatlantic partnership.

Instead, the new German national identity will be anchored more firmly within Europe, perhaps even expanded toward the East. After all, European politics has always had a special status in German foreign policy thought and certainly continues to do so.[49] This does not mean that Germany will abandon its *Westpolitik* completely – as suggested in the introduction, the land of middle cannot afford to do so –, but it may change the dynamics between old partners. At any rate, the United States should not expect Germans to continue falling in line automatically, despite the recent "Joint Declaration Renewing the Transatlantic Partnership" that was signed by prominent U.S. representatives on May 14th, 2003, and well received in Europe.

In the Bundestag debates analyzed in this book, the rhetoric of the political elite supports the above arguments. German politicians' talk about the European Union and European interests as opposed to Germany and German interests are perhaps indicative of a transformation of national identity toward a supranational European identity. There is evidence in the debates that German policy makers are beginning to think more in "European terms."

Table 5.6: Frequencies of "Germany," "Europe," "America," "NATO"

	Kosovo *8 Debates*	Afghanistan *8 Debates*	*Iraq* *3 Debates*	Total *19 Debates*
Germany	506	309	248	**1063**
Europe	282	229	271	**782**
America	74	378	182	**634**
NATO	323	120	60	**503**

Compared to how frequently the members of the Bundestag spoke of Germany, the talk about Europe has been catching up during the four years observed here, suggesting that Europe and European issues were a matter of great interest in the political debates. Not only did German politicians talk about Europe often, they also spoke of it in highly positive terms. And while the speakers were reluctant to address "German interests," they showed no such hesitation when speaking of "European interests." Although the talk about the United States also become more frequent in the debates, it should be noted that it also became more negative and openly critical, beginning in the Afghanistan debates and culminating in the Iraq debates.

It is too early to say whether this indicates a change in Germans national identity, but it certainly does not indicate a return to nationalist ideals. Much will depend on the political elite's efforts of "social engineering," i.e. the conscious promotion of a common European identity.[50] It seems possible that the recent clash of interests/ideologies between Europe and the United States could promote further European integration and the perceptions of European unity among citizens. Despite "statements that there is no European identity for which people are willing to make sacrifices," it must be kept in mind that "European identity will not be important only if it out-competes the national identities – and until then remain irrelevant. 'Europe' *is* important for the way the national identities have been reshaped."[51]

How German National Interests Have Changed

> *I'm sure you have heard that Germany has reunited. The only question now, I guess, is when it will go on tour again.*
> – Jay Leno, The Tonight Show

Germany's interests and how it pursues them have changed since – and because of – the devastating experience of World War II. Even after the end of the Cold War, Germans are hesitant to act in a manner befitting Germany's position of power, and they certainly do not like to talk about power or the pursuit of national interests in their political or public debates.

The total number of times German politicians talked about interests in the debates examined here are fairly insignificant when compared to the frequencies of other, more idealist concepts, such as responsibility, peace, freedom, and human rights. Nonetheless, Germans have become slightly more comfortable talking about their interests, even their national interests to a degree, between the first and the last case analyzed here. In the Kosovo debates, only 23% of all talk about interests referred to specifically German interests, whereas the rest referred to either European interests or the interests of the refugees and Kosovar-Albanians. It seems reasonable to assume that in 1999 German leaders were afraid of the potential effects on their neighbors should they emphasize national interests as a motivation for the intervention in Kosovo. Not only was this the first time that German troops participated in an actual combat mission, but the intervention also occurred in a region where memories of the Wehrmacht's activities were still very much alive.

Two years later, almost 57% of all interest talk during the Afghanistan debates referred to German interests. In particular, the members of the Bundestag spoke of the need to respond to the invocation of NATO's Article 5 as being in Germany's national interest, due to the fact that NATO remains critical to Germany's security. To a lesser degree, German interests were seen as being at stake in the war against terrorism, though there never was any talk of specific interests that would be served by intervening in Afghanistan other than the restoration of international stability. It is questionable whether Germans really perceived the September 11th attacks as a direct threat to their own country, or whether they were merely responding to the enormity of the event. Finally, the fact that this mission was largely supported by the international community, was sanctioned both by NATO and United Nations, and was taking place in a part of the world that is not associated with the events of World War II, probably made it easier for the Bundestag to talk about German interests without fearing that it would give cause for concern.

During the Iraq debates, German interests accounted for 35% of all talk about interests. This represents a decline from the Afghanistan debates, but still a definite rise compared to Kosovo. More important perhaps than Germans interests is the talk about European interests in the case of Iraq, which is much more frequent than either in Kosovo or Afghanistan. This is noteworthy because it might be seen as evidence that Germans are increasingly thinking in European terms and are perhaps even beginning to equate European interests with German interests. This finding further strengthens the above arguments about German and European identity. Bundestag members clearly felt authorized to speak on behalf of Europe in the Iraq debates.

Nonetheless, talk of responsibility and democratic commitment as justification for German behavior still far outweighed talk about interests in all three cases. Does that mean that interests are not determining factors, or does it merely mean that talk is cheap and German policy makers are using idealist rhetoric in order to mask their true intentions, but it is national interest that drives German foreign policy?

The answer is that national interests are the guiding principles of German foreign policy, but they cannot explain everything! Throughout the Cold War, German interests and the dominant discourse of historical memory did not clash. After the Cold War had ended, Germany's external environment had changed so much that suddenly the two most important variables in its foreign policy – interests and historical memory – had become incompatible, necessitating a compromise between the two. The generational effect allowed German elites to begin reinterpreting the lessons of history in such a way that it enabled them to reconcile the pursuit of national interests with German historical memory. Nonetheless, certain constraints still apply, which is why one cannot speak of a purely interest-based foreign policy.

The ambivalence in the debates accompanying the deployment of German troops suggests that the power of historical memory – or at least the version that demands a reticent foreign policy – is still strong enough to constrain German behavior. After all, the constitutional debate during the mid-1990s about the Bundeswehr showed that the limitations on participation in military interventions have been mainly ideological rather than institutional. Then and now, Germans could choose to practice a more assertive foreign policy and to increase the deployment of troops in number and scope, yet they continue to choose not to!

It is true that Germany is more likely to pursue its national interests in the 21st century, but only within institutional contexts and never alone! The debates have clearly shown this. While there may be some room for interpretation as to which institutional context is considered acceptable and exactly what constitutes multilateralism, this does prevent a return to unilateralist power politics. In addition, these particular lessons of history have become so entrenched in German foreign policy thought that they are likely to remain a significant influence as a result of a path-dependency.

Implications for the Future of German Foreign Policy

In the 21st century, German foreign policy will become more self-assured and pragmatic as the country continues to mature in the wake of far-reaching generational changes that allow the questioning of more and more traditional taboos, such as the use of military force. The literature of path-dependency suggests, however, that this process will be incremental in nature rather than occur in a rash and dramatic fashion. The influence of historical memory will remain strong enough to prevent a return to unilateralist power politics for a long time to come, though the dominant discourse of collective memory will increasingly become challenged by more pragmatic versions.

Germany will intensify its efforts to promote European integration, not only – or even primarily – because it is one of the lessons of history, but because it has come to be seen as in Germany's best interest as well. First priority will be given to the deepening of *Kerneuropa* (core

Europe), followed by the widening of the union by admitting new members from Eastern Europe and even Turkey. Germans have learned the hard way that attempting to secure their interests in the region through aggressive military force will never be crowned with success. Instead, Germany has begun to rely on soft power within the institutional framework of the European Union, thus achieving two of its primary, geopolitically motivated goals: security and influence. By putting on the golden handcuffs, the German problem has been solved, as even the smaller member states of the European Union have begun to trust Germany once again.

Because German foreign policy priorities will always lie in Europe, there is the potential for a deeper rift between Germany and the United States, if disagreements over fundamental issues such as the war on terrorism and its methods are not resolved. The continuation of the special friendship between the two countries is threatened by several circumstances: (1) the generational effect in Germany weakens feelings of gratitude and solidarity with the United States for the help received during and after World War II; (2) geopolitical changes following the end of the Cold War have produced divergent interests on both sides of the Atlantic; (3) Europe does not have the same strategic importance for the United States as it did before the collapse of the Soviet Union. Instead, the United States has become more focused on the Middle East in the war against terrorism, whereas Germany's priorities have been defined as lying within Europe. NATO has thus far served as the glue that held Europe and America together, but that may not be the case forever.

The current crisis in Iran should be considered a test for Europe's ability to persist in its emancipation from the United States. In that context, it will be of significant importance to plan and implement a common European course of action, perhaps under the leadership of a more confident Germany. This should happen in cooperation with the United States, if possible, but not at any price. If cooperation requires a continuation of the quasi lord-vassal relationship of the past, then Germany should push for a more independent European policy. Naturally this would require a reform of the German/European armed forces as well, mainly in the form of overcoming Europe's inferiority in the areas of strategic mobility and command and control systems. This is in the European Union's – and therefore Germany's – best interest, because in the face of the above mentioned geopolitical changes, Europe can no longer depend on the United States' military protection.

Germany is in a unique position to use the lessons of its negative past for a positive future. There is a clearly discernible longing for change among the German population, a new underlying optimism on which the political elite could and should capitalize in order to promote a new vision for the 21st century. During the 2006 Soccer World Cup in Germany, the German public agreed that a team does not win games through defensive play. Even the political elite praised the new German national coach's model (*Modell Klinsmann*), which was characterized by independence, self-confidence, and optimism. Perhaps Germany's leadership could learn something from its national coach in that respect. Germany's primary foreign policy goal is spelled out in the preamble to the Basic Law: "To promote peace in the world as an *equal* member in a unified Europe" (emphasis added!).

---

[1] In an interview with Steve Crawshaw, in: "A Nation Faces its Demons," *The Independent*, London, July 13, 2004.

[2] For a detailed treatment of the 'Munich Analogy' from an American perspective, see Yueng Foong Khong (1992). *Analogies at War: Korea, Munich, Dien Bien Phu, and the Vietnam Decisions of 1965.* Princeton, NJ: Princeton University Press.

[3] This had been a pillar of German foreign policy thinking throughout the Cold War and during the early 1990s, so the interpretation in the Iraq debates constituted more of a return to old interpretations than a reinterpretation of the lessons of history.

[4] Ole Wæver, for instance, argued that "whenever an actor is unable to fulfill the dual criteria of compatibility with both structures, it will have to try to modify one of them, the one that is least rigid ... This leads occasionally to quite drastic reorientations of policy, when a situation has suddenly become unstable due to the squeeze from these two sets of structures," in: Ole Wæver (2003). *European Integration and National Identity: Analysing French and German Discourses on State, Nation, and Europe,* p. 11.

[5] Of course this does not necessarily apply to a more general, collective guilt that is perpetuated through institutions and through electronic media as the new carriers of memory. Cf. Siobhan Kattago (2001). *Ambiguous Memory: The Nazi Past and German National Identity.* Westport, CT: Praeger, p. 18.

[6] Klaus Neumann (2000). *Shifting Memories: The Nazi Past in the New Germany.* Ann Arbor, MI: University of Michigan Press; Geoffrey H. Hartman, ed., (1986). *Bitburg in Moral and Political Perspective.* Bloomington, IN: Indiana University Press; Eric Langenbacher (2003). "Changing Memory Regimes in Contemporary Germany?" *German Politics and Society* (June).

[7] Stephen F. Szabo (2004). "The Return of the German Problem," *The Globalist,* February 17, 2004 (http://www.theglobalist.com); John J. Mearsheimer (2003). *The Tragedy of Great Power Politics.* New York, NY: Norton; Charles Lees (2001). *The Red-Green Coalition in Germany: Politics, Personalities and Power.* New York: Manchester University Press.

[8] NOTE: there may be an unobserved variable bias: compared to previous years, the 15th Bundestag also had a much larger number of members from the

Green party, which is known for its extremely liberal and pacifist beliefs; in addition, it had the largest number of female members, who might arguably also be more inclined toward diplomatic solutions

[9] A possible alternative explanation could be found in Ronald Inglehart's argument that advanced industrial societies embrace postmodernist values, de-emphasizing the instrumental rationality that characterized industrial society. As such, the modern German belief system could be partly an expression of postmodern sensibilities. See Ronald Inglehart and Christian Welzel (2005). *Modernization, Cultural Change, and Democracy: The Human Development Sequence.* New York, NY: Cambridge University Press.

[10] Jörg Friedrich (2002). *Der Brand: Deutschland im Bombenkrieg 1940-1945.* Berlin: Propyläen Verlag.

[11] Günther Grass (2002). *Im Krebsgang: Eine Novelle.* Göttingen: Steidl (translated into English in 2003 as *Crabwalk*).

[12] See Alexander Mitscherlich and Margarete Mitscherlich (2004). *Die Unfähigkeit zu trauern: Grundlagen kollektiven Verhaltens.* Munich: Piper; the authors argue that Germans found it difficult to mourn their own losses after World War II, because to do so would have required a level of acceptance of the consequences of their actions that would have been too painful. In contrast, the admission of collective guilt allowed a more impersonal responsibility. See also: Ralph Giordano (2000). *Die Zweite Schuld oder Von der Last Deutscher zu Sein.* Cologne: Kiepenheuer & Witsch.

[13] Günther Grass, *Im Krebsgang*, p. 29.

[14] See Friedemann Schmidt (2001). *Die Neue Rechte und die Berliner Republik.* Wiesbaden: Verlag für Sozialwissenschaften.

[15] Bettina Westle (2002). *Kollektive Identität im vereinten Deutschland. Nation und Demokratie in der Wahrnehmung der Deutschen.* Wiesbaden: Leske + Budrich, p. 71.

[16] Esther B. Fein (1992). "Günther Grass Considers the Inescapable: Politics," Dember 29, 1992, *The New York Times* http://www.nytimes.com/ books/99/12/19/specials/grass-inescapable.html).

[17] Based on an online opinion poll carried out by GEO, a popular German science magazine, in 2003 (http://www.geo.de/GEO/kultur/geschichte/ 2864.html?q=geschichte%20weltkrieg%20umfrage).

[18] Translated by author.

[19] Adam Krzeminski (2003). "Die schwierige deutsch-polnische Vergangenheitspolitik," *Aus Politik und Zeitgeschichte*, B 40-41/2003, p. 3.

[20] Lorenz Jäger (2002). "Das Böse," *Frankfurter Allgemeine Zeitung*, November 28, 2002.

[21] See Peter Reichel (1995). *Politik mit der Erinnerung.* Munich: Carl Hanser Verlag; Wolfgang Benz, ed., (2004). *Wann ziehen wir endlich den Schlussstrich?* Berlin: Metropol Verlag.

[22] For a detailed study on the clash between the two camps see Aleida Assmann and Ute Frevert (1999). *Geschichtsvergessenheit–Geschichtsver- essenheit: Vom Umgang mit der deutschen Vergangenheit nach 1945.* Stuttgart: DVA.

[23] Die Debatte um den Film "Der Untergang" (http://www.3ndr.de).

[24] This is true both for the political elite and for the general public, according to an opinion poll carried out by FORSA in 2004.

[25] See Andres Prüfert, ed., (2003). *Hat die allgemeine Wehrpflicht in Deutschland eine Zukunft? Zur Debatte um die künftige Wehrstruktur.* Baden-Baden: Nomos; Eckhardt Opitz and Frank S. Rödiger, eds., (1995). *Allgemeine Wehrpflicht: Geschichte, Probleme, Perspektiven.* Bremen: Edition Temmen; Karl Haltiner (1998). "The Definite End of the Mass Army in Western Europe?" *Armed Forces and Society*, vol. 25, no. 1 (Fall), pp. 7-36.

[26] Hans-Jürgen Leersch, "Eine Armee des Volkes und der Demokratie," *Die Welt*, June 8, 2005, p. 5.

[27] *Ibid.*

[28] Geoffrey van Orden (1991). "The Bundeswehr in Transition," *Survival*, vol. 33 (July/August), p. 239.

[29] Steve Crenshaw (2004). "Germany's New Normality," *Spiegel Online*, December 23, 2004 (http://www.spiegel.de).

[30] Ute Frevert (2003). Geschichtsvergessenheit und Geschichtsversessenheit revisited," *Aus Politik und Zeitgeschichte*, B 40-41, p. 7.

[31] *Frankfurter Rundschau*, January 22, 1998.

[32] Harald Welzer, Sabine Moller, and Karoline Tschugnall, eds., (2002). *Opa war kein Nazi: Nationalsozialismus und Holocaust im Familiengedächtnis.* Frankfurt: Fischer.

[33] Steven Ozment (2004). *A Mighty Fortress: A New History of the German People.* New York, NY: HarperCollins, p. 13.

[34] Jeffrey Anderson (2002). "The New Germany in the New Europe," published by the American Foreign Service Association (http://www.afsa.org/fsj/sept01/Andersonsept01.cfm, downloaded on August 24, 2005).

[35] Dirk Verheyen (1999). *The German Question: A Cultural, Historical, and Geopolitical Exploration.* Boulder, CO: Westview Press, p. 34.

[36] I should note that I do not mean to excuse past actions – especially during the reign of the Nazis – as the result of the mere desire to feel more secure. However, it is undeniable that geopolitical and security considerations have always played a dominant role in German foreign policy.

[37] In: Dallek, Robert (1995). Franklin D. Roosevelt and American Foreign Policy, 1932-1945. Oxford Oxfordshire: Oxford University Press, p. 475.

[38] U.S. Occupation Directive JCS 1779.

[39] Treaty on the Final Settlement with Respect to Germany, September 12, 1990.

[40] See Jeffrey S. Lantis (2002). *Strategic Dilemmas and the Evolution of German Foreign Policy since Unification.* Westport, CT: Praeger; Max Otte (2000). *A Rising Middle Power? German Foreign Policy in Transformation, 1989-1999.* New York: St. Martin's Press; Siobhan Kattago (2001). *Ambiguous Memory: The Nazi Past and German National Identity.* Westport, CT: Praeger.

[41] François Furet and Ernst Nolte (1991). *Fascism and Communism.* Lincoln, NE: University of Nebraska Press; Elizabeth Noelle-Neumann and Renate Köcher, eds., (1987). *Die verletzte Nation – Über den Versuch der Deutschen, ihren Charakter zu ändern.* Stuttgart: Deutsche Verlagsanstalt; W. Weidenfeld (1993). "Deutschland nach der Vereinigung," in: W. Werner, ed., *Deutschland: Eine Nation, doppelte Geschichte.* Cologne: Verlag Wissenschaft und Politik, pp. 13-26.

[42] Jürgen Habermas (1989). *The New Conservativism: Cultural Criticism and the Historian's Debate.* Cambridge: MA: MIT Press; M. Greiffenhagen (1991). "Die Bündesrepublik Deutschland 1945-1990," in: *Aus Politik und Zeitgeschichte*, B1-2, pp. 16-26; Ralf Dahrendorf (1992). *Betrachtungen über die Revolution in Europa.* Bergisch-Gladbach.

[43] D. Oberndörfer (1991). *Die offene Republik – Zur Zukunft Deutschlands und Europa.* Freiburg; H. Kleger (1994). "Reflexive Politikfähigkeit – Zur Verschränkung von Bürger- und Staatsgesellschaft," in: J. Gebhardt und R. Schmalz-Bruns, eds., *Demokratie, Verfassung und Nation*, Baden-Baden, pp. 301-319.

[44] Despite predictions to the contrary, such as Günther Grass' pessimistic statement that German reunification would be tantamount to a new *Anschluss*. Compare also Harold James and M. Stone, eds. (1992). *When the Wall Came Down: Reactions to German Unification.* New York: Routledge.

[45] Bettina Westle (2002). *Kollektive Identität im vereinten Deutschland. Nation und Demokratie in der Wahrnehmung der Deutschen.* Wiesbaden: Leske + Budrich.

[46] This source of national pride has remained relatively stable ever since then: see Gabriel A. Almond and Sidney Verba (1963). *The Civic Culture.* Princetown, NJ: Princeton University Press; David Conradt (1996). *The German Polity.* White Plains, NY: Longman.

[47] Christian Hacke (1993). *Weltmacht wider Willen: Die Außenpolitik der Bundesrepublik Deutschland.* Berlin: Ullstein, p. 538; Josep R. Llobera (1994). *The God of Modernity: The Development of Nationalism in Western Europe.* Oxford: Berg.

[48] Gregor Schöllgen (2004). "Die Zukunft der deutschen Außenpolitik liegt in Europa," in: *Aus Politik und Zeitgeschichte*, B 11, pp. 9-16 (translation: The future of German foreign policy lies in Europe).

[49] Gisela Müller-Brandeck-Bocquet, ed., (2002). *Deutsche Europapolitik von Konrad Adenauer bis Gerhard Schröder.* Opladen; Heinrich Schneider, Matthias Jopp, and Uwe Schmalz, eds., (2001). *Eine neue Europapolitik? Ramenbedingungen – Problemfelder – Optionen.* Bonn.

[50] See Jürgen Habermas (2002). "Toward a European Political Community," *Society*, July/August; Benedict Anderson (1983). *Imagined Communities.* London: Verso; Geoffrey Garrett and Barry R. Weingast (1993) "Ideas, Interests, and Institutions: Constructing the European Community's Internal Market," in: *Ideas and Foreign Policy: Beliefs, Institutions, and Political Change*, edited by Judith Goldstein and Robert O. Keohane. Ithaca, N.Y.: Cornell University Press, pp. 173-206.

[51] Ole Wæver, Ulla Holm, and Henrik Larsen (2004). *The Struggle for 'Europe': French and German concepts of state, nation and European Union.*

Acronyms

CDU	Christian Democratic Union
CSU	Christian Social Union
EU	European Union
FDP	Free Democratic Party
FRG	Federal Republic of Germany
FRY	Former Republic of Yugoslavia
GDR	German Democratic Republic
IFOR	Implementation Force
KLA	Kosovar Liberation Army
NATO	North Atlantic Treaty Organization
PDS	Party of Democratic Socialism
RAF	Red Army Faction
SFOR	Stabilization Force
SPD	Social Democratic Party
UN	United Nations
UNAMIC	United Nations Advance Mission in Cambodia
UNOMIG	United Nations Observer Mission in Georgia
UNOSOM II	United Nations Operation in Somalia II
UNPROFOR	United Nations Protection Force
UNTAG	United Nations Transition Assistance

Bibliography

Primary Sources

Kosovo Debates:

Deutscher Bundestag, Plenarprotokoll 13/248, 13. Wahlperiode, 248. Session, 10/16/1998

Deutscher Bundestag, Plenarprotokoll 14/6, 14. Wahlperiode, 6. Session, 11/13/1998

Deutscher Bundestag, Plenarprotokoll 14/8, 14. Wahlperiode, 8. Session, 11/19/1998

Deutscher Bundestag, Plenarprotokoll 14/22, 14. Wahlperiode, 22. Session, 02/25/1999

Deutscher Bundestag, Plenarprotokoll 14/30, 14. Wahlperiode, 30. Session, 03/25/1999

Deutscher Bundestag, Plenarprotokoll 14/31, 14. Wahlperiode, 31. Session, 03/26/1999

Deutscher Bundestag, Plenarprotokoll 14/32, 14. Wahlperiode, 32. Session, 04/15/1999

Deutscher Bundestag, Plenarprotokoll 14/40, 14. Wahlperiode, 40. Session, 05/07/1999

Afghanistan Debates:

Deutscher Bundestag, Plenarprotokoll 14/186, 14. Wahlperiode, 186. Session, 09/12/2001

Deutscher Bundestag, Plenarprotokoll 14/187, 14. Wahlperiode, 187. Session, 09/19/2001

Deutscher Bundestag, Plenarprotokoll 14/186, 14. Wahlperiode, 186. Session, 09/12/2001

Deutscher Bundestag, Plenarprotokoll 14/189, 14. Wahlperiode, 189. Session, 09/26/2001

Deutscher Bundestag, Plenarprotokoll 14/192, 14. Wahlperiode, 192. Session, 10/11/2001

Deutscher Bundestag, Plenarprotokoll 14/195, 14. Wahlperiode, 195. Session, 10/18/2001

Deutscher Bundestag, Plenarprotokoll 14/198, 14. Wahlperiode, 198. Session, 11/08/2001

Deutscher Bundestag, Plenarprotokoll 14/202, 14. Wahlperiode, 202. Session, 11/16/2001

Deutscher Bundestag, Plenarprotokoll 14/210, 14. Wahlperiode, 210. Session, 12/22/2001

Iraq Debates:

Deutscher Bundestag, Plenarprotokoll 15/25, 15. Wahlperiode, 25. Session, 02/13/2003
Deutscher Bundestag, Plenarprotokoll 15/35, 15. Wahlperiode, 35. Session, 03/20/2003
Deutscher Bundestag, Plenarprotokoll 15/37, 15. Wahlperiode, 37. Session, 04/03/2003
Bulletin des Presse- und Informationsamtes der Bundesregierung, 1/95

Secondary Sources

Adenauer, Konrad (1949). "First Government Statement," delivered on September 20, 1949, in: *Außenpolitik der Bundesrepublik Deutschland: Dokumente von 1949 bis 1994*, 170-175.

Almond, Gabrial A., and Sidney Verba (1963). *The Civic Culture*. Princetown, NJ: Princeton University Press.

Almond, Gabrial A., and Sidney Verba (1989). *The Civic Culture Revisited*. Newbury Park, CA: Sage Publications.

Alter, Reinhard, and Peter Monteath (1997). *Rewriting the German Past: History and Identity in the New Germany*. Atlantic Highlands, NJ: Humanities Press.

Anderson, Jeffrey (2002). "The New Germany in the New Europe," published by the *American Foreign Service Association* (http://www.afsa.org/fsj/sept01/Andersonsept01.cfm, downloaded on August 24, 2005).

Anderson, Jeffrey J., and John B. Goodman (1993). "Mars or Minerva: A United Germany in a Post-Cold War Europe," in Robert O. Keohane, Joseph S. Nye, and Stanley Hoffmann, eds., *After the Cold War*. Cambridge, MA: Harvard University Press, 23-63.

Asmus, Ronald (1993). The Future of German Strategic Thinking," in: Gary Geipel, ed., *Germany in a New Era*. Indianapolis, IN: The Hudson Institute.

Assmann, Aleida, and Ute Frevert (1999). *Geschichtsvergessenheit – Geschichtsversessenheit: Vom Umgang mit der deutschen Vergangenheit nach 1945*. Stuttgart: DVA.

Bach, Jonathan P. G. (1999). *Between Sovereignty and Integration: German Foreign Policy and National Identity after 1989*. New York, NY: St. Martin's Press.

Bahr, Egon (1999). "Die Normalisierung der deutschen Außenpolitik: Mündige Partnerschaft statt bequemer Vormundschaft," *Internationale Politik*, vol 54, no. 1, 41-52.

Bahr, Egon (2003). *Der deutsche Weg: Selbstverständlich und normal*. Munich.

Balleck, Barry J., and Francis A. Beer (1994). "Realist/Idealist Texts: Psychometry and Semantics". *Peace Psychology Review* 1, 38-44.

Banchoff, Thomas F. (1999). *The German Problem Transformed: Institutions, Politics, and Foreign Policy, 1945-1995*. Ann Arbor, MI: University of Michigan Press.

Banerjee, Sanjoy (1996). "Constructivism in International Studies: Cognitive Science, Interaction, and Narrative Structure." Paper presented at the International Studies Organization, April 16-20, San Diego, California.

Barber, Benjamin R. (2003). *Fear's Empire: War Terrorism, and Democracy.* New York: W. W. Norton & Co.

Baring, Arnulf (1994). "Germany, What Now?" in: *Germany's New Position in Europe*, edited by A. Baring. Oxford: Berg.

Barzel, Rainer (1968). *Gesichtspunkte eines Deutschen. Düsseldorf*, Germany: Econ-Verlag.

Baumann, Rainer, and Gunther Hellmann (2001). "Germany and the Use of Military Force: 'Total War', the 'Culture of Restraint' and the Quest for Normalcy," in Douglas Webber, ed., *New Europe, New Germany, Old Foreign Policy?* Portland, OR: Frank Cass, 61-83.

Beer, Francis A. (1994). "Words of Reason". *Political Communication* 11, 185-201.

— —. (2001). *Meanings of War and Peace.* College Station, TX: Texas A&M University Press.

Beer, Francis A., and Robert Hariman, eds., (1996). *Post-Realism: The Rhetorical Turn in International Relations.* East Lansing, MI: Michigan State University Press.

Beer, William R., and James E. Jacob (1986). *Language Policy and National Unity.* Totowa, NJ: Rowman & Allanheld.

Bennett, Milton. J., ed., (1998). *Basic Concepts of Intercultural Communication.* Yarmouth, Maine: Intercultural Press Inc.

Benz, Wolfgang, ed., (2004). *Wann ziehen wir endlich den Schlusstrich?* Berlin: Metropol Verlag.

Berger, Stefan (1997). *The Search for Normality: National Identity and Historical Consciousness in Germany since 1800.* Providence/Oxford: Berghan Books.

Berger, Thomas (1996). "Norms, Identity, and National Security in Germany and Japan," in: Peter J. Katzenstein, ed., *The Culture of National Security*, New York: Columbia University Press.

— — (1998). *Cultures of Antimilitarism: National Security in Germany and Japan.* Baltimore, MD: John Hopkins University Press.

— — (1999). "The Burdens of Memory: The Impact of History on German National Security Policy," in: John S. Brady, Beverly Crawford, and Sarah Elise Wiliarty. *The Postwar Transformation of Germany.* Ann Arbor, MI: The University of Michigan Press: 473-503.

Berndt, Michael (1997). *Deutsche Militärpolitik in der neuen 'Weltordnung'. Zwischen nationalen Interessen und globalen Entwicklungen.* Münster: Lit Verlag.

von Bernstorff, Graf Johann-Heinrich (1920). *Deutschland und Amerika: Erinnerungen aus dem fünfjährigen Kriege.* Berlin.

Bork, Dennis L., and David R. Gress (1989). *A History of West Germany: From Shadow to Substance 1945-1963.* Oxford: Blackwell.

Borsche, Tilman, ed., (1996). *Klassiker der Sprachphilosophie: von Platon bis Chomsky.* München: Verlag C. H. Beck.

Bracher, Karl Dietrich, ed., (1982). *Deutscher Sonderweg: Mythos oder Realität?* Munich.

Brockmann, Stephen (1996). "Germany at the 'Zero Hour'," in: *Revisiting Zero Hour 1945: The Emergence of Postwar Culture*, edited by S. Brockmann. Washington, D.C.: AICGS.

Brunner, Jerome (1991) "The narrative construction of reality", *Critical Inquiry*, Vol. 18, No. 2, 1-21.
Buck, Carl Darling (1916). "Language and the Sentiment of Nationality," *The American Political Science Review*, Volume 10, Issue 1, 44-69.
Burger, Rudolf (2001). "Die Politik der moralischen Militärintervention," in: Konrad Paul Liessmann, ed., *Der Vater aller Dinge: Nachdenken über den Krieg*. Wien, 118-137.
Carr, David (1986). *Time, Narrative, and History*. Bloomington, Indiana: Indiana University Press.
Carver, T., and Hyvärinen, M., eds., (1997). *Interpreting the Political: New Methodologies*. New York: Routledge.
Carver, Terrell (2002). "Discourse Analysis and the 'Linguistic Turn'" Symposium Discourse Analysis & Political Science, European Consortium for Political Research.
Cioffi-Revilla, Claudio (1998). *Politics and Uncertainty: Theory, Models, and Applications*. Cambridge, NY: Cambridge University Press.
Clemens, Clay (1993). "A Special Kind of Superpower? Germany and the Demiltarization of Post-Cold War International Security," in: Gary Geipel, ed., *Germany in a New Era*. Indianapolis, IN: The Hudson Institute.
Conradt, David P. (1996). *The German Polity*. White Plains, NY: Longman.
Corcoran (1990). "Language and Politics," in: Swanson, David L., and Dan Nimmo (1990). *New Directions in Political Communication: A Resource Book*. Newbury Park, CA: Sage.
Coste, Didier (1989). *Narrative and Communication*. Minneapolis: University of Minneapolis Press.
Craig, Gordon A. (1971). *Europe since 1815*. Harcourt College Publication.
Crawshaw, Steve (2004). "A Nation Faces its Demons," *The Independent*, London, July 13, 2004.
— — (2004). "Germany's New Normality," *Spiegel Online*, December 23, 2004 (http://www.spiegel.de).
Czempiel, Ernst-Otto. (2002). *Weltpolitik im Umbruch: Die Pax Americana, der Terrorismus und die Zukunft der international Beziehungen*. Munich.
Dallek, Robert (1995). *Franklin D. Roosevelt and American Foreign Policy, 1932-1945*. Oxford: Oxford University Press.
Derrida, Jacques (1976). *Of Grammatology*. Translated by G. C. Spivak. Baltimore: Johns Hopkins University Press.
Diez, Thomas (1999). *Die EU lesen: Diskursive Knotenpunkte in der britischen Europadebatte*, Opladen: Leske & Budrich.
Donoghue, Denis (1976). *The Sovereign Ghost: Studies in Imagination*. Berkeley, CA: University of California Press.
Duffield, John S. (1998). *World Power Forsaken: Political Culture, International Institutions, and German Security Policy after Unification*. Stanford, CA: Stanford University Press.
Eckstein, Harry (1988). "A Culturalist Theory of Political Change," *American Political Science Review*, Vol. 82, No. 3 (September), 789-804.
Elshtain, Jean-Bethke (1995). "Feminist Themes and International Relations," in: James der Derian, ed., *International Theory: Critical Investigations*. London: Macmillan.
Erb, Scott (2003). *German Foreign Policy: Navigating a New Era*. Boulder, CO: Lynne Rienner Publishers.

Erhardt, Ludwig (1963). "First Government Statement," delivered on October 18, 1963, in: *Außenpolitik der Bundesrepublik Deutschland: Dokumente von 1949 bis 1994,* 281-83.

Erikson, Kai (1966). *Wayward Puritans: A Study in the Sociology of Deviance.* New York, NY: Wiley.

Eschenburg, Theodor (1983). *Jahre der Besatzung 1945-1949.* Stuttgart: Deutsche Verlagsanstalt.

Evans, Richard J. (1989). *Im Schatten Hitler's? Historikerstreit und Vergangenheitsbewältigung in der Bundesrepublik.* Frankfurt: Edition Suhrkamp.

Esther B. Fein (1992). "Günther Grass Considers the Inescapable: Politics," December 29, 1992, *The New York Times* (http://www.nytimes.com/books/ 99/12/19/specials/grass-inescapable.html).

Finnemore, Martha (1996). *National Interests in International Society.* Ithaca, NY: Cornell University Press.

Fishman, Joashua A. (1989). *Language and Ethnicity in Minority Sociolinguistic Perspective.* Clevedon, Philadelphia: Multilingual Matters Ltd.

Fishman, Joshua A., ed., (1999). *Handbook of Language and Ethnic Identity.* New York, NY: Oxford University Press.

Fishman, Joshua A., et. al. (1985). *The Rise and Fall of the Ethic Revival: Perspectives on Language and Ethnicity.* New York, NY: Mouton Publishers.

Fiske, Susan T., and Shelly E. Taylor (1984) *Social Cognition.* Reading, MA: Addison-Wesley Publications.

Ford, Gerald (1979). *A Time to Heal.* New York: Harper & Row.

Foucault, Michael (1984). "The Order of Discourse," in: Michael Shapiro, ed., *Language and Politics.* New York: New York University Press.

Frevert, Ute (2003). Geschichtsvergessenheit und Geschichtsversessenheit revisited," *Aus Politik und Zeitgeschichte,* B 40-41, 6-14.

Friedrich, Jörg (2002). *Der Brand: Deutschland im Bombenkrieg 1940-1945.* Berlin: Propyläen Verlag.

Fulbrook, Mary (1999). *German National Identity after the Holocaust.* Oxford: Polity.

Furet, François, and Ernst Nolte (1991). *Fascism and Communism.* Lincoln, NE: University of Nebraska Press.

Gardt, Andreas, Ulrike Hass-Zumkehr, and Thorsten Roelcke, eds., (1999). *Sprachgeschichte als Kulturgeschichte.* Berlin: De Gruyter.

Garrett, Geoffrey, and Barry R. Weingast (1993) "Ideas, Interests, and Institutions: Constructing the European Community's Internal Market," in: *Ideas and Foreign Policy: Beliefs, Institutions, and Political Change,* edited by Judith Goldstein and Robert O. Keohane. Ithaca, N.Y.: Cornell University Press.

Geertz, Clifford (1973). *The Interpretation of Cultures: Selected Essays.* New York, NY: Basic Books.

Giesen, Bernhard, ed., (1991). *Nationale und kulturelle Identität.* Frankfurt a.M.: Suhrkamp.

— —, ed., (1993). *Die Intellektuellen und die Nation.* Frankfurt a. M.: Suhrkamp.

Gilpin, Robert (1981). *War and Change in World Politics.* New York: Cambridge University Press.

Giordano, Ralph (2000). *Die Zweite Schuld oder Von der Last Deutscher zu Sein.* Cologne: Kiepenheuer & Witsch.

Glaser, Hermann (1991). *Kleine Kulturgeschichte der Bundesrepublik Deutschland 1945-1989.* Bonn: Bundeszentrale für Politische Bildung.

Glees, Anthony (1996). *Reinventing Germany: German Political Development Since 1945.* Dulles, VA: Berg.

Glotz, Peter (1994). *Die falsche Normalisierung. Essays.* Frankfurt am Main: Suhrkamp.

Goldhagen, Daniel (1996). *Hitler's Willing Executioners: Ordinary Germans and the Holocaust.* New York, NY: Knopf.

Goldstein, Judith, and Robert O. Keohane (1993). *Ideas and Foreign Policy: Beliefs, Institutions, and Political Change.* Ithaca, NY: Cornell University Press.

Gonzalez, Alberto, and Dolores V. Tanno, eds., (1997). *Politics, Communication, and Culture.* Thousand Oaks, CA: SAGE Publications.

Grass, Günther (2002). *Im Krebsgang: Eine Novelle.* Göttingen: Steidl.

Grebing, H., ed., (1986). *Der 'deutsche Sonderweg' in Europa 1806-1945: Eine Kritik.* Stuttgart: W. Kohlhammer.

Greener, Ian (2005). "The Potential of Path Dependence in Political Studies," *Politics*, Vol. 25, No. 1, 62-72.

Gries, Peter Hays (2004). *China's New Nationalism: Pride, Politics, and Diplomacy.* Berkeley, CA: University of California Press.

Gries, Rainer (1991). *Die Rationen-Gesellschaft: Versorgungskampf und Vergleichmentalität.* Leipzig: Westfalisches Dampfboot, 210-13.

Grin, Francois (1999). "Economics," in: Joshua A. Fishman (ed.). *Handbook of Language and Ethnic Identity.* New York, NY: Oxford University Press.

Gross, Johannes (1993). "Notizbuch Johannes Gross. Neueste Folge," *FAZ-Magazin*, 26 February 1993.

Grossmann, Atina (2000). "The 'Goldhagen Effect': Memory, Repetition, and Responsibility in the New Germany," in: Geoff Eley, ed., *The "Goldhagen" Effect: History, Memory, Nazism – Facing the German Past.* Ann Arbor, MI: University of Michigan Press.

Guelke, Adrian (1993). *The Age of Terrorism and the International Political System.* New York: St. Martin's Press.

Haar, Roberta N. (2001). *Nation States as Schizophrenics: Germany and Japan as Post-Cold War Actors.* Westport, CT: Praeger.

Haarmann, Harald (1986). *Language in Ethnicity: A View of Basic Ecological Relations.* New York, NY: Mouton de Gruyter.

Habermas, Jürgen (1989). *The New Conservativism: Cultural Criticism and the Historian's Debate.* Cambridge: MA: MIT Press.

— — (1994). *Vergangenheit als Zukunft: Das alte Deutschland im neuen Europa?*, translated by Max Pensky as *The Past as Future*, Cambridge, MA: Polity Press.

— — (1998). *A Berlin Republic: Writings on Germany.* Cambridge: Polity Press.

— — (2001). *Zeit der Übergänge.* Frankfurt a. M.: Suhrkamp;

— — (2002). "Toward a European Community," *Society*, July/August, 58-61.

Habermas, Jürgen, and Jacques Derrida (2003). "February 15, Or What Binds Europeans Together: A Plea for a Common Foreign Policy, Beginning in the Core of Europe," *Constellations*, Vol. 10, No. 3, 291-297.

Hacke, Christian (1993). *Weltmacht wider Willen: Die Außenpolitik der Bundesrepublik Deutschland*. Berlin: Ullstein.

Hajer, Maarten A. (1993). "Discourse coalitions and the Institutionalisation of Practice. The case of acid rain in Britain," in: J. Forester and F. Fischer, eds., *The Argumentative Turn in Policy and Planning*, Durham, NC: Duke University Press, 43-76.

Halbwachs, Maurice (1992). *On Collective Memory*. Chicago: The University of Chicago Press.

Hallerbach, Rolf (1991). "Zauberformel der Zukunft: Multinationale NATO-Truppen," *Europäische Sicherheit*, 40:1, 21-23.

Haltiner, Karl (1998). "The Definite End of the Mass Army in Western Europe?", *Armed Forces and Society*, Vol. 25, No. 1 (Fall), 7-36.

Harbecke, Ulrich (1999). *Abenteuer Deutschland: Von der Bonner zur Berliner Republik*. Bergisch Gladbach: Gustav Lübbe Verlag.

Harlan, David (1989). "Intellectual History and the Return of Literature," *American Historical Review*, Vol. 94, 581-609.

Harnisch, Sebastian, and Hanns M. Maull (2001). *Germany as a Civilian Power? The Foreign Policy of the Berlin Republic*. New York, NY: Palgrave.

Hartman, Geoffrey H., ed., (1986). *Bitburg in Moral and Political Perspective*. Bloomington, IN: Indiana University Press.

Hasenclever, Andreas, Peter Mayer, and Volker Rittberger (1009). *Theories of International Regimes*. Cambridge, MA: Cambridge University Press.

Hastedt, Glen P. (2006). *American Foreign Policy: Past, Present, Future*. Upper Saddle River, NJ: Pearson Prentice Hall.

Hauser, Gerard (1999). *Vernacular Voices: The Rhetoric of Publics and Public Spheres*. Columbia: University of South Carolina Press.

Hellmann, Gunther (1998). "Die prekäre Macht: Deutschland an der Schwelle zum 21. Jahrhundert," in: Wolf-Dieter Eberwein und Karl Kaiser, eds., *Deutschlands neue Außenpolitik, Vol. 4: Institutionen und Ressourcen*. Munich: Oldenbourg, 265-82.

Hellmann, Gunther (1999). "Nationale Normalität als Zukunft? Zur Außenpolitik der Berliner Republik," *Blätter für deutsche und international Politik*, Vol. 44, No. 7, 837-47.

Heneghan, Tom (2000). *Unchained Eagle: Germany after the Wall*. Financial Times Prentice Hall.

Hoffmann, Lutz (1994). *Das deutsche Volk und seine Feinde: die völkische Droge*. Cologne: PapyRossa Verlag.

Hoffmann, Stanley (1995). "Reflections on the German Question," in: *The European Sisyphus: Essays on Europe, 1964-1994*. Boulder, CO: Westview Press.

Hofstede, Geert (1980). *Culture's Consequences*. Beverly Hills, CA: Sage.

Holsti, Olè (1969). *Content Analysis in the Social Sciences and Humanities*. Reading, MA: Addison-Wesley Publications.

Horchem, Hans Joseph (1991). "The Terrorist Lobby in Germany: Campaigns and Propaganda in Support of Terrorism," in: Noemi Gal-Or, ed.,

Tolerating Terrorism in the West: An International Survey. New York: Routledge.

Horowitz, Donald L. (2000). *Ethnic Groups in Conflict*. Second Edition. Berkeley, CA: University of California Press.

Hudson, Valerie M., ed., (1997). *Culture and Foreign Policy*. Boulder, CO: Lynne Rienner Publishers.

Hyde-Price, Adrian (1999). "Berlin Republic Takes to Arms," *The World Today*, (June).

—— (2001). "Germany and the Kosovo War: Still a Civilian Power?" in: Douglas Webber, ed., *New Europe, New Germany, Old Foreign Policy?* Portland, OR: Frank Cass.

Ikenberry, G. John, ed., (2002). *America Unrivalled: The Future of the Balance of Power*. Ithaca, NY: Cornell University Press.

Inglehart, Ronald, and Christian Welzel (2005). *Modernization, Cultural Change, and Democracy: The Human Development Sequence*. New York, NY: Cambridge University Press.

Jäger, Lorenz (2002). "Das Böse," *Frankfurter Allgemeine Zeitung*, November 28, 2002.

Jakobeit, Cord, Ute Sackofsky, and Peter Welzel, eds., (1996). *The United States and German-American Relations through German Eyes*. Commack, NY: Nova Science Publishers.

James, Harold, and M. Stone, eds. (1992). *When the Wall Came Down: Reactions to German Unification*. New York: Routledge.

James, Peter (1998). *Modern Germany: Politics, Culture, and Society*. London: Routledge.

Jamieson, Karlyn, and Kathleen Campbell (1990). *Deeds done in Words*: *Presidential Rhetoric and the Genres of Governance*. Chicago, IL: University of Chicago Press.

Joetze, Günter (2001). *Der letzte Krieg in Europa? Das Kosovo und die deutsche Politik*. München: DVA.

Jonas, Manfred (1984). *The United States and Germany*. Ithaca, NY: Cornell University Press.

Kagan, Robert (2003). *Of Paradise and Power: America and Europe in the New World Order*. New York: Knopf.

Kalyvas, Stathis N. (1996). *The Rise of Christian Democracy in Europe*. Ithaca, NY: Cornell University Press.

Kattago, Siobhan (2001). *Ambiguous Memory: The Nazi Past and German National Identity*. Westport, CT: Praeger.

Katzenstein, Peter J. (1996b). *Cultural Norms and National Security: Police and Military in Postwar Japan*. Ithaca, NY: Cornell University Press.

——, ed., (1996a). *The Culture of National Security: Norms and Identity in World Politics*. New York: Columbia University Press.

——, ed., (1997). *Tamed Power: Germany in Europe*. Ithaca, NY: Cornell University Press.

Keohane, Robert O., and Stanley Hoffmann (1991). *The New European Community: Decision-Making and Institutional Change*. Boulder, CO: Westview Press.

Keohane, Robert O., Joseph S. Nye, and Stanley Hoffmann (1993). *After the Cold War: International Institutions and State Strategy in Europe 1989-1991*. Cambridge, MA; Harvard University Press.

Khong, Yuen Foong (1992). *Analogies at War*. Princeton, NJ: Princeton University Press.

Kielinger, Thomas. "Der Golf-Krieg und die Folgen aus deutscher Sicht," *Außenpolitik* 42 (3), 241-250

Kirchen (2003). "Präventiver Krieg," *Frankfurter Allgemeine Zeitung*, February 6, 2003.

Kitfield, James (2004). "Of Politics and Power: The Deepening Transatlantic Divide is More about Power Politics than Cultural Trends or a Perceived 'Values' Gap," *American Institute for Contemporary German Studies* (http://www.aicgs.org), downloaded on March 1, 2006.

Kitschelt, Herbert (1994). *The Transformation of European Social Democracy*. New York, NY: Cambridge University Press.

Klotz, Audie (1995). *Norms in International Relations: The Struggle Against Apartheid*. Ithaca, NY: Cornell University Press.

Krzeminski, Adam (2003). "Die schwierige deutsch-polnische Vergangenheitspolitik," *Aus Politik und Zeitgeschichte*, B 40-41/2003, 3-6.

Kühnl, Reinhard (1987). "The German Sonderweg Reconsidered: Continuities and Discontinuities in Modern German History," in: *Rewriting the German Past*, edited by P. Monteath and R. Alter. Atlantic Highlands, NJ: Humanities Press

Küntzel, Matthias (2000). *Der Weg in den Krieg: Deutschland, die Nato und das Kosovo*. Berlin: Elefanten Press.

Laclau, Ernesto, and Chantal Mouffe (1985) *Hegemony and Socialist Strategy: Towards a radical democratic politics*, London: Verso.

Langenbacher, Eric (2003). "Changing Memory Regimes in Contemporary Germany?" *German Politics and Society* (June).

Lankowski, Carl, ed., (1999). *Breakdown, Breakup, Breakthrough: Germany's Difficult Passage to Modernity*. New York: Berghahn Books.

Lankowski, Carl. ed., (1993). *Germany and the European Community: Beyond Hegemony and Containment?* New York: St. Martin's Press.

Lantis, Jeffrey S. (2002). *Strategic Dilemmas and the Evolution of German Foreign Policy since Unification*. Westport, CT: Praeger.

Laqueur, Walter (1999). *The New Terrorism: Fanaticism and the Arms of Mass Destruction*. New York, NY: Oxford University Press.

Larsen, Henrik (1997). *Foreign Policy and Discourse Analysis: France, Britain, and Europe*. New York, NY: Routledge.

Lasswell, H. D. (1951). "The Policy Orientation," in H. D. Lasswell and D. Lerner, eds., *The Policy Sciences: Recent Developments in Scope and Method*. Stanford CA: Stanford University Press.

Layne, Christopher (1993). "The Unipolar Illusion: Why New Great Powers Will Rise," *International Security* 17:4, 5-51.

Leersch, Hans-Jürgen, "Eine Armee des Volkes und der Demokratie," *Die Welt*, June 8, 2005.

Lees, Charles (2001). *The Red-Green Coalition in Germany: Politics, Personalities and Power*. New York: Manchester University Press.

Lepgold, Joseph (1998). "NATO's Post-Cold War Collective Action Problem," *International Security*, Vol. 23, No. 1 (Summer) 1998, 78-106.

Levi, Margaret (1997). "A Model, a Method, and a Map: Rational Choice in Comparative and Historical Analysis," in: Mark I. Lichbach and Alan S.

Zuckerman, eds., *Comparative Politics; Rationality, Culture, and Structure*. Cambridge, UK: Cambridge University Press.

Link, Werner (2004). "Grundlinien der außenpolitischen Orientierung Deutschlands," in: *Aus Politik und Zeitgeschichte*, B11/2004, 3-8

Llobera, Josep R. (1994). *The God of Modernity: The Development of Nationalism in Western Europe*. Oxford: Berg.

Loquai, Heinz (2000). *Der Kosovo-Konflikt . Wege in einen vermeidbaren Krieg. Die Zeit von Ende November 1997 bis März 1999*. Baden-Baden.

Loquai, Heinz (2003). "Medien als Weichensteller zum Krieg," *Referat während der Sommerakademie auf Burg Schlaining* (Austria).

Macmillan, Alan (1995). "Strategic Culture and National Ways in Warfare: The British Case," *RUSI Journal* (October).

Majone, G. (1989). *Evidence, Argument, and Persuasion in the Policy Process*. New Haven CT: Yale University Press.

March, James G., and Johan P. Olsen (1989*). Rediscovering Institutions: The Organizational Basis of Politics*. New York: Free Press.

Markovits, Andrei S., and Simon Reich (1999). "The Contemporary Power of Memory: The Dilemmas for German Foreign Policy," in: John S. Brady, Beverly Crawford, and Sarah Elise Wiliarty. *The Postwar Transformation of Germany: Democracy, Prosperity, and Nationhood*. Ann Arbor, MI: The University of Michigan Press, 439-473.

Maull, Hanns W. (1992). "Zivilmacht Bundesrepublik Deutschland – Vierzehn Thesen für eine neue deutsche Außenpolitik," *Europa Archiv*, 43:10, 269-78.

McAdams, A. James (1997). Review Article "Germany after Unification: Normal at Last?" *World Politics* 49:2, 282-308.

McCloskey, Donald N. (1985). *The Rhetoric of Economics*. Madison: Wisconsin University Press.

McElroy, Robert W. (1992). Morality and American Foreign Policy: The Role of Ethics in International Affairs. Princeton, NJ: Princeton University Press.

Mearsheimer, John J. (1990). "Back to the Future: Instability in Europe after the Cold War," *International Security* 15:1, 5-56.

— — (1995). "The False Promise of International Institutions," *International Security* 19:3, 5-49.

— — (2003). *The Tragedy of Great Power Politics*. New York, NY: Norton.

Merkl, Peter (1986). *Political Violence and Terror*. Berkley, CA: University of California Press.

Mertes, Michael, Steven Müller, and Heinrich August Winkler, eds. (1996). *In Search of Germany*. New Brunswick, NJ: Transaction Publishers.

Meyer, Berthold, and Peter Schlotter (2000). *Die Kosovo-Kriege 1998/99. Die internationalen Interventionen und ihre Folgen*. HSFK-Report 1/2000. Frankfurt/M.

Milliken, Jennifer (1999). "The Study of Discourse in International Relations: A Critique of Research and Methods," *European Journal of International Relations* 5:2, 225-254.

Millotat, Christian (1996). "NATO and Germany: A Renaissance in Strategy," *Parameters*, 26:1, 51-61.

Mitscherlich, Alexander, and Margarete Mitscherlich (2004). *Die Unfähigkeit zu trauern: Grundlagen kollektiven Verhaltens*. Munich: Piper.

Moravscik, Andrew (1998). *The Choice for Europe: Social Purpose and State Power from Messina to Maastricht.* Ithaca, NY: Cornell University Press.

Morgenthau, Hans (1948). *Politics Among Nations.* New York: Knopf.

Müller-Brandeck-Bocquet, Gisela, ed., (2002). *Deutsche Europapolitik von Konrad Adenauer bis Gerhardt Schröder.* Opladen.

Mushaben, Joyce Marie (1998). *From Post-War to Post-Wall Generations : Changing Attitudes Toward the National Question and NATO in the Federal Republic of Germany.* Boulder, CO: Westview Press.

Mutz, Reinhard (1993). "Schießen wie die anderen? Eine Armee sucht ihren Zweck," in: Dieter S. Lutz, ed., *Deutsche Soldaten weltweit? Blauhelme, Eingreiftruppen, 'out-of area' – Der Streit um unsere sicherheitspolitische Zukunft.* Reinbeck: Rowohlt, 11-26.

Narr, Wolf-Dieter, Roland Roth, and Klaus Vack (1999). *Wider die kriegerischen Menschenrecht:. Eine pazifistisch-menschenrechtliche Streitschrift. Beispiel: Kosovo 1999 – NATO-Krieg gegen Jugoslawien.* Komitee für Grundrechte und Freiheiten, Köln.

Neack, Laura, Jeanne A. K. Hey, and Patrick J. Haney (1995). *Foreign Policy Analysis: Continuity and Change in its Second Generation.* Englewood Cliffs, NJ: Prentice Hall.

Neidhardt, Friedhelm (1982). "Linker und rechter Terrorismus. Erscheinungsformen und Handlungspotentiale im Gruppenvergleich," in: Wanda von Baeyer-Katte et al., *Gruppenprozesse.* Opladen: Westdeutscher Verlag, 433-476.

Nelson, B. (1996). "Public Policy and Administration: An Overview," in R. E. Goodin and H.-D. Klingemann, eds., *A New Handbook of Political Science.* Oxford: Oxford University Press.

Neumann, Klaus (2000). *Shifting Memories: The Nazi Past in the New Germany.* Ann Arbor, MI: University of Michigan Press.

Ninkovich, Frank (1995). *Germany and the United States: The Transformation of the German Question since 1945.* New York: Twayne Publishers.

Noelle-Neumann, Elizabeth, and Renate Köcher, eds., (1987). *Die verletzte Nation – Über den Versuch der Deutschen, ihren Charakter zu ändern.* Stuttgart: Deutsche Verlagsanstalt.

Nolte, Ernst (1987). "Between Myth and Revisionism? The Third Reich in the Perspective of the 1980s," in: Erich Nolte and Michael Stürmer, eds., *Historikerstreit.* Munich: Piper.

O'Reilly, Camille (2001). *Language, Ethnicity and the State.* New York, NY: Palgrave.

Oliverio, Annamarie (1998). *The State of Terror.* Albany, NY: State University of New York Press.

Opitz, Eckhardt, and Frank S. Rödiger, eds., (1995). *Allgemeine Wehrpflicht: Geschichte, Probleme, Perspektiven.* Bremen: Edition Temmen.

van Orden, Geoffrey (1991). "The Bundeswehr in Transition," *Survival,* Vol. 33, No. (July/August).

Otte, Max (2000). *A Rising Middle Power? German Foreign Policy in Transformation, 1989-1999.* New York: St. Martin's Press.

Ozment, Steven (2004). *A Mighty Fortress: A New History of the German People.* New York, NY: HarperCollins.

Padilla, Amado (1999). "Psychology," in: Joshua A. Fishman (ed.). *Handbook of Language and Ethnic Identity.* New York, NY: Oxford University Press.

Phillipson, Robert (1999). "Political Science," in: Joshua A. Fishman (ed.). *Handbook of Language and Ethnic Identity*. New York, NY: Oxford University Press.

Pierson, Paul (1993). "When Effect Becomes Cause: Policy Feedback and Political Change," *World Politics*, Vol. 45, No. 4.

Pinson, Koppel S. (1954). *Modern Germany: Its History and Civilizations*. New York: The Macmillan Company.

Pleasants, N. (1999). *Wittgenstein and the Idea of a Critical Social Theory: A Critique of Giddens, Habermas and Bhaskar*. London: Routledge.

Pradetto, August (2004). "From 'Tamed' to 'Normal' Power: A New Paradigm in German Foreign and Security Policy?" in: Reutter, ed., *Germany on the Road to 'Normalcy': Policies and Politics of the Red-Green Federal Government (1998-2002)*." New York, NY: Palgrave, Macmillan, 209-235.

Prüfert, Andres, ed., (2003). *Hat die allgemeine Wehrpflicht in Deutschland eine Zukunft? Zur Debatte um die künftige Wehrstruktur*. Baden-Baden: Nomos.

Putnam, Robert (1993). *Making Democracy Work: Civic Traditions in Modern Italy*. Princeton: Princeton University Press.

Rau, Johannes (2003). "Gemeinsam handeln: Deutschlands Verantwortung in der Welt," in: *Bulletin*, Nr. 41/1, May 19, 2005.

Reichel, Peter (1995). *Politik mit der Erinnerung*. Munich: Carl Hanser Verlag.

Reutter, Werner, ed., (2004). *Germany on the Road to 'Normalcy': Policies and Politics of the Red-Green Federal Government (1998-2002)*." New York, NY: Palgrave, Macmillan.

Ricœur, Paul (1990). *Time and Narrative: Volume I*. Chicago, IL: University of Chicago Press.

— — (1995) "Reflections on a New Ethos for Europe" in *Philosophy & Social Criticism*, 21, No 5-6, 3-14.

— — (2004). *Memory, History, and Forgetting*. Chicago, IL: University of Chicago Press.

von Rimscha, Robert (2004). "The Deepest Ocean after the German-American Clash over Iraq: Cultural and Generational Dimensions of the Transatlantic Rift," *American Institute for Contemporary German Studies* (http://www.aicgs.org), downloaded on March 1, 2006.

Risse, Thomas (2004). "Kontinuität durch Wandel: Eine 'neue' deutsche Außenpolitik?," *Aus Politik und Zeitgeschichte*, B11/2004.

Rittberger, Volker, and Wolfgang Wagner (2001). "German Foreign Policy since Unification: Theories Meet Reality," in Volker Rittberger, ed., *German Foreign Policy since Unification*. Manchester, UK: Manchester University Press.

Rittberger, Volker, ed., (2001). *German Foreign Policy since Unification: Theories and Case Studies*. Manchester, UK: Manchester University Press.

Rosati, Jerel A. (1995). "A Cognitive Approach to the Study of Foreign Policy," in *Foreign Policy Analysis: Continuity and Change in its Second Generation*, edited by Laura Neack, Patrick J. Haney, and Jeanne A.K. Hey. Englewood Cliffs, NJ: Prentice-Hall, 49-70.

— — (2000). "The Power of Human Cognition in the Study of World Politics," *International Studies Review*, Vol. 2, No. 3 (Autumn), 45-75.

Rosecrance, Richard N. (1986). *The Rise of the Trading State: Commerce and Conquest in the Modern World*. New York: Basic Books.

Rosen, Stephen P. (1995). "Military Effectiveness: Why Society Matters," *International Security*, Vol. 19, No. 4 (Spring).

Ross, James C. (2002). *Talking Immigration: A Rhetorical Analysis of U.S. Senate Debates, 1924 – 1965 – 1996.* Doctoral Thesis, University of Colorado at Boulder.

Rubino-Hallman, Silvana (1998). "Representations of the Gulf Crisis as derived from the U.S. Senate debate," in: Donald Sylvan and James Voss (1998). *Problem Representation in Foreign Policy Decision Making.* Cambridge, NY: Cambridge University Press.

Rühe, Volker (1996). "Growing Responsibility," *German Comments*, No. 42 (April).

Safran, William (1999). "Nationalism," in: Joshua A. Fishman, (ed.). *Handbook of Language and Ethnic Identity.* New York, NY: Oxford University Press.

Scharping, Rudolf (1999). *Wir dürfen nicht wegsehen. Der Kosovo-Krieg und Europa.* Berlin.

Schmidt, Friedemann (2001). *Die Neue Rechte und die Berliner Republik.* Wiesbaden: Verlag für Sozialwissenschaften.

Schmiese, Wulf (2000). *Fremde Freunde. Deutschland und die USA zwischen Mauerfall und Golfkrieg.* Paderborn.

Schneider, Heinrich, Matthias Jopp, and Uwe Schmalz, eds., (2001). *Eine neue Europapolitik? Ramenbedingungen – Problemfelder – Optionen.* Bonn.

Schöllgen, Gregor (1993). *Angst vor der Macht: Die Deutschen und ihre Außenpolitik.* Berlin: Ullstein.

Schöllgen, Gregor (2004). "Die Zukunft der deutschen Außenpolitik liegt in Europa," *Aus Politik und Zeitgeschichte*, B11/2004, 9-16.

Schulze, Hagen (1998). *Germany: A New History.* Cambridge, MA: Harvard University Press.

Schwan, Gesine (2001). *Politics and Guilt: The Destructive Power of Silence.* Lincoln, NE: University of Nebraska.

Seeßlen, Georg (1999). "Kriegsnovelle oder Wie eine Erzählgemeinschaft für einen moralischen Krieg erzeugt wird," in: Klaus Bittermann und Thomas Deichmann, eds., *Wie Dr. Joseph Fischer lernte, die Bombe zu lieben.* Berlin.

Sereny, Gitta (2001). *The Healing Wound: Experiences and Reflections on Germany, 1938-2001.* New York: W. W. Norton & Company.

Shapiro M. J. (1985-86), "Metaphor in the Philosophy of the Social Sciences", *Culture and Critique*, 2, 191-214

Smyser, W. R. (1999). *From Yalta to Berlin: The Cold War Struggle over Germany.* New York: St. Martin's Griffin.

Staack, Michael (2000). *Handelsstaat Deutschland: Deutsche Außenpolitik in einem neuen internationalen System.* Paderborn, Germany: Schöning.

Stent, Angela E. (1999). *Russia and Germany Reborn: Unification, the Soviet Collapse, and the New Europe.* Princeton, NJ: Princeton University Press.

Sternberger, Dolf (1990). *Verfassungspatriotismus.* Schriften Bd. X. Frankfurt a. M.: Suhrkamp.

Stürmer, Michael (1992). *Die Grenzen der Macht.* Berlin: Siedler Verlag

Sundhaussen, Holm (2000). "Kosovo: Eine Konfliktgeschichte," in: Konrad Clewing and Jens Reuter, eds.: *Der Kosovo-Konflikt: Ursachen – Akteure – Verlauf.* Bayerische Landeszentrale für politische Bildung: München, 65-88.

Swanson, David L., and Dan Nimmo (1990). *New Directions in Political Communication: A Resource Book.* Newbury Park, CA: Sage.

Sylvan, Donald, and James Voss (1998). *Problem Representation in Foreign Policy Decision Making.* Cambridge, NY: Cambridge University Press.

Szabo, Stephen F. (2004). "The Return of the German Problem," *The Globalist,* February 17, 2004 (http://www.theglobalist.com).

Thatcher, Margaret (1993). *The Downing Street Years.* Harper Collins.

Torfing, Jacob (1999). *New theories of discourse: Laclau, Mouffe and Žižek,* Oxford: Blackwell.

Valentin, Veit (1984). *Die Geschichte der Deutschen.* Droemer Knaur.

Verheyen, Dirk (1999). *The German Question: A Cultural, Historical, and Geopolitical Exploration.* Boulder, CO: Westview Press.

Vertzberger, Yacoov (1990). *The World in Their Minds: Information Processing, Cognition, and Perception in Foreign Policy Decision-Making.* Stanford, CA: Stanford University Press.

Wæver, Ole (1996). "Discourse Analysis as Foreign Policy Theory: The case of Germany and Europe," http://www.ciaonet.org/wps/wao01/.

Wæver, Ole, Ulla Holm, and Henrik Larsen (2004). *The Struggle for 'Europe': French and German concepts of state, nation and European Union.*

Waltz, Kenneth N. (1993). "The Emerging Structure of International Politics," *International Security* 18:2, 44-79.

Wardhaugh, Ronald (1998). *An Introduction to Sociolinguistics.* Third Edition. Malden, MA: Blackwell Publishers.

Webber, Douglas, ed., (2001). *New Europe, New Germany, Old Foreign Policy? German Foreign Policy since Unification.* Portland, OR: Frank Cass.

Weidenfeld, W. (1993). "Deutschland nach der Vereinigung," in: W. Werner, ed., *Deutschland: Eine Nation, doppelte Geschichte.* Cologne: Verlag Wissenschaft und Politik, 13-26.

Weldes, Jutta (1999). *Constructing National Interests: The United States and Cuban Missile Crisis.* Minneapolis, MN: University of Minnesota Press.

Welzer, Harald, Sabine Moller, and Karoline Tschugnall, eds., (2002). *Opa war kein Nazi: Nationalsozialismus und Holocaust im Familiengedächtnis.* Frankfurt: Fischer.

Wendt, Alexander (1999). *Social Theory of International Politics.* New York: Cambridge University Press.

Westle, Bettina (2002). *Kollektive Identität im vereinten Deutschland. Nation und Demokratie in der Wahrnehmung der Deutschen.* Wiesbaden: Leske + Budrich.

White, H. (1987). *The Content of the Form: Narrative Discourse and Historical Representation.* Baltimore MD: Johns Hopkins University Press.

Willett, Ralph (1989). *The Americanization of Germany, 1945-1949.* New York: Routledge.

Wolffsohn, Michael (1993). *Eternal Guilt? Forty Years of German-Jewish-Israeli Relations.* New York: Columbia University Press.

Wolfgang Wessels (2001). "Germany's Power and the Weakening of States in a Globalised World: Deconstructing a Paradox," in Douglas Webber, *New Europe, New Germany, Old Foreign Policy? German Foreign Policy since Unification.* Portland, OR: Frank Cass.

Yee, Albert S. (1997). "Thick Rationality and the Missing 'Brute Fact'," *Journal of Politics* 59 (November), 1001-1050.

Zelikow, Philip, and Condoleezza Rice (1995). *Germany Unified and Europe Transformed: A Study in Statecraft.* Cambridge, MA: Harvard University Press.

Zimmer, Matthias, ed., (1997). *Germany: Phoenix in Trouble?* Edmonton, Alberta, Canada: University of Alberta Press.

Index

About the Book

Reconciling the imperatives of Germany's national identity and its national interest has been a challenge for the country's policymakers since the end of the Cold War. Anika Leithner explores how (and how much) the past continues to shape Germany's foreign policy behavior in the first decade of the twenty-first century.

Leithner argues that, while German foreign policy is still heavily influenced by the memory of World War II, the exact nature of that memory is slowly changing as the lessons of history are being reinterpreted. Focusing on the military interventions in Kosovo, Afghanistan, and Iraq, she deftly illustrates the ways in which the lessons of history have been manipulated in the pursuit of an assertive foreign policy—one that can appease audiences at home while securing a leadership role for Germany in Europe and beyond.

Anika Leithner is assistant professor of political science at California Polytechnic State University.

I